Grammar Sense 4

TEACHER'S BOOK

Catharine Dalton

OXFORD

UNIVERSITY PRESS

UNIVERSITY PRESS

198 Madison Avenue
New York, NY 10016 USA

Great Clarendon Street
Oxford OX2 6DP England

Oxford New York

Auckland Cape Town Dar es Salaam Hong Kong Karachi
Kuala Lumpur Madrid Melbourne Mexico City Nairobi
New Delhi Shanghai Taipei Toronto
With offices in
Argentina Austria Brazil Chile Czech Republic France Greece
Guatemala Hungary Italy Japan Poland Portugal Singapore
South Korea Switzerland Thailand Turkey Ukraine Vietnam

OXFORD and OXFORD ENGLISH are registered trademarks of Oxford University Press

Editorial Director: Sally Yagan
Publishing Manager: Kenna Bourke
Associate Editor: Scott Allan Wallick
Production Manager: Shanta Persaud
Production Controller: Soniya Kulkarni

ISBN: 978 0 19 449038 2

Printed in Hong Kong

10 9 8 7 6 5 4 3

Contents

Teacher's Book Introduction
Catharine Dalton

About the Teacher's Book

THE CHAPTERS

- **Overview:** Each chapter of the Teacher's Book begins with an overview of the grammar presented in the Student Book chapter. It enables the teacher to focus on the main points covered in the chapter, and highlights difficulties students may have with the structures.

- **Grammar in Discourse:** This section provides directions to help the teacher teach the Before You Read, Read, and After You Read activities in the Student Book. It suggests creative ways to activate background knowledge, offers innovative reading strategies, and gives tips on checking comprehension.

- **Form, Meaning, and Use:** This section offers advice on teaching the inductive Examining Meaning and Use exercises. It includes a variety of suggested techniques for mastering the rules and examples contained in the Meaning and Use Notes. Teachers are also provided with ideas for making efficient use of the charts through pair and group work.

- **Trouble Spots:** These notes, placed at strategic points throughout the Teacher's Book, alert the teacher to problems that students may have with the grammar. They suggest how to address these problems effectively, and, where relevant, direct the teacher to parts of the Student Book that clarify or offer practice of the grammar point.

- **Cultural Notes:** These occasional notes give background about American culture that students typically do not know, and that may help their understanding of the topic in the Student Book. The teacher can relay this information to students as appropriate.

- **Writing:** This section offers suggestions for helping students internalize common errors for the target grammar points, and directions for helping the instructor teach the editing sections. It then moves to ideas on how to present Beyond the Sentence sections. These are model texts showing students how grammatical structures are used in combination in extended written discourse.

- **Additional Activities:** The Student Book provides extensive practice of each grammatical structure. However, for teachers who want to give further practice, each Teacher's Book chapter contains at least one additional writing or speaking activity.

AT THE BACK OF THE BOOK

- **Student Book Tapescript:** A complete tapescript is available for every listening activity in the Student Book.

- **Student Book Answer Key:** The Teacher's Book contains the answers to all the Student Book exercises. (The answers are not available in the Student Book.)

Teaching Techniques for the Grammar Classroom

TEACHING STUDENTS AT THE ADVANCED LEVEL

Students at this level will have already been exposed to most of the forms as well as some of the meanings and uses of the structures presented in the Student Book. They may still need to focus on form issues in more complex clauses and verb phrases, such as word order, agreement, and multiple auxiliary verbs. They may also be interested in the finer details of meaning and use, such as the distinction between the present perfect and present perfect continuous, the use of stative verbs in continuous forms, or the subtle differences in meaning and use between gerunds and infinitives. *Grammar Sense 4* provides students at this level with the necessary guidance and a wealth of exercises to practice and expand their grammar knowledge.

Examining Form Exercises

One of the most challenging aspects of teaching grammar is finding clear and concise ways to present new forms to students. The Examining Form exercise in each chapter is a series of inductive tasks in which students work on identifying the target structure and its most important structural features. In these exercises, students are asked to return to the reading text in the Grammar in Discourse section of the chapter, and follow the steps to recognize or systematically analyze key aspects of the form (such as the number of different parts in a structure, the addition of suffixes, word order, agreement, and so on). This serves as an introduction to the structural features illustrated and explained in the Form, Meaning, and Use Notes, which students may then consult.

PRESENTING THE FORM, MEANING, AND USE SECTIONS

Examining Meaning and Use Exercises

Once students have grasped the form of a given structure, the next challenge is to find creative and engaging ways to help them understand the meaning and use. The Examining Meaning and Use exercises do just this by offering carefully constructed examples, often in the form of minimal pairs, and asking students to use contextual cues to draw inferences about key aspects of meaning and use. These inductive tasks serve as an introduction to the features of meaning and use that are further elucidated in the Notes that follow.

Form, Meaning, and Use Notes

Students need to read and absorb the Form, Meaning, and Use Notes before starting the exercises. What follows are some techniques for helping students work through the Form, Meaning, and Use Notes. Regardless of the technique presented, it is important that you have a clear understanding of the scope of the Form, Meaning, and Use Notes before you present them. In some instances, a particular structure may have multiple meanings and uses, but the chapter may not address all of them. In Levels 1–3, certain meanings and uses of structures are omitted to avoid overwhelming the students with too much information, while in Level 4, basic meanings and uses may be de-emphasized in order to focus on more complex issues.

- **Correlating notes:** To reinforce the information presented in the Note, have students correlate the example sentences to the explanations in bullets. This can be done as a writing exercise, speaking practice, and as individual or pair work. Follow-up questions are provided to assist in checking for comprehension.

- **Writing new examples:** Students can practice using the new structure by modeling new example sentences on those featured in the Notes. Students should be referred to the bulleted explanations in the Notes before receiving explicit assistance in constructing the structure. Students may compose their sentences in pairs or individually and then exchange work for peer editing.

- **Deconstructing form:** The information in the Notes may first be presented in isolation on the board as class activity, allowing for students to ask questions and discuss the structure.

The structure is presented on the board with books closed and then analyzed relative to the form, meaning, and use of the structure. Follow-up exercises, such as writing new examples, assist in checking for comprehension.

- **Practice with elicitation:** Students are first introduced to the structure through elicitation. Key follow-up questions are provided to help students understand the use of the structure after being introduced to the structure. The practice may be extended with a writing or boardwork exercise.

- **Peer teaching:** First students are asked to read the Notes and to discuss any questions briefly as a class. Students are then split into small groups and told to study a specific portion of the Notes. Each group will present their information to the rest of the class in the form of a summary and with additional examples that they create.

PRESENTING THE WRITING SECTIONS

These sections allow you to guide students in applying what they have learned about the target structure(s) to academic writing.

Editing

Editing sections train students in ways of avoiding common errors. First students are asked to study the errors in the Editing box. While the initial Editing presentation can be done as a class, the following editing exercises should be done individually to help simulate an authentic self-editing situation that students will encounter. When examples with errors are provided to present to students, they are noted with an asterisk (*).

Beyond the Sentence

Students need to see how target structures work in combination in extended discourse before beginning the writing task. The Beyond the Sentence section provides students with a model paragraph or paragraphs, featuring callout boxes which highlight the uses of the target structures. Students are thus able to see the connection between what they have learned in the Form, Meaning, and Use sections and academic writing.

Writing

The section continues with a Writing Tip. This is intended to answer the question: why learn this particular grammatical structure? Before tackling an extended writing assignment, students are given an explanation of the practical application of the target structure to academic writing. There then follows a selection of writing topics that students can choose from in order to write their own essays. Writing is best done individually in class or as homework. Students are also provided with a Writing Checklist to encourage self-editing.

General Teaching Techniques

Grammar Sense contains a wealth of exercises covering all four skills areas: reading, writing, listening, and speaking. Depending on your students, curriculum, and time frame, these exercises can be taught in many ways. Successful grammar teaching requires skillful classroom management and teaching techniques, especially in the areas of elicitation (drawing information from students), grouping procedures (groups, pairs, or individuals), time management (lengthening or shortening exercises), and error correction (peer or teacher correction, correction of spoken or written errors).

ELICITATION

Elicitation is one of the most useful teaching techniques in the grammar classroom. In essence, elicitation draws information out of the students through the use of leading questions. This helps students to discover, on their own, information about grammar forms as well as meanings and uses. For example, to elicit the difference in meaning between a gerund and an infinitive when used after the verb *stop*, write the following sentences on the board: *Alan stopped to smoke before he entered the building. Alan stopped smoking because of his health.* Then, in order to elicit the difference in meaning between the two sentences, ask questions such as, *In which sentence are we talking about a smoker? Which sentence is about a reformed (or ex-) smoker?* These questions require students to analyze what they know about the grammar in context and to make inferences about meaning.

Knowing when to elicit information can be difficult. Too much elicitation can slow the class and too little elicitation puts students in a passive position. Avoid asking students to judge whether something sounds natural or acceptable to them because, as non-native speakers, they will not have the same intuitions about English as native speakers.

GROUPING STUDENTS

Group work is a valuable part of language learning. It takes away the focus from the teacher as the provider of information and centers on the students, giving them the opportunity to work together and rely on each other for language acquisition. Shyer students who may be less likely to speak out in class have an opportunity to share answers or ideas. Your class level will inform how you approach group work. Be sure to circulate among groups to monitor the progress of an activity, particularly at lower levels, and to answer any questions students cannot resolve on their own. Although students at the higher levels are more independent and can often manage their own groups, be attentive to the activities at hand, ready to offer feedback and keep everyone on-task. In classes where the level of students is uneven, try varying the composition of the groups to make the learning process interesting for everybody. Sometimes you can pair up a higher-level student with a lower-level student to give him or her an opportunity to help another classmate. However, other times you may want to group all the higher-level students together and offer them additional, more challenging activities. It is useful, especially in discussion activities, to conclude with a culminating task in which one or more students report back something (results, a summary) to the rest of the class using the target structure. This helps to refocus the class on the structure and provide a conclusion to the activity.

TIME MANAGEMENT

Some exercises are divided into steps, making it possible to shorten an activity by assigning part of it for homework or by dividing the class into two groups and assigning half the items to each group. Similarly, exercises can be lengthened. Many of the exercises in *Grammar Sense* require students to ask for or offer real-life information. You can ask students to create additional sentences within these activities, or have them do an activity again with a different partner. If your class does an activity well, ask them to focus on other aspects of the form, for example, transforming their affirmative sentences into negative ones, and vice-versa.

CHECKING EXERCISES

How you check exercises with students will depend on the level you are teaching. Having students check their answers in pairs or groups can be an effective technique, because it makes students revisit their work and resolve with other students the mistakes they have made. With lower levels, this requires careful teacher supervision. It is also possible at all levels to check exercises as a class, elicit corrections from students, and offer necessary feedback. It is often useful, especially for correcting editing exercises, to use an overhead projector. Be careful not to single out students when correcting work. Aim instead to create a supportive atmosphere whereby the class learns through a group effort.

CORRECTING ERRORS

Students can often communicate effectively without perfect grammar. However, in order to succeed in higher education or the business world, they need to demonstrate a high level of grammatical accuracy, and to understand that even a small change in form can sometimes result in a significant change in meaning. As students become aware of this, they expect to be corrected. However, their expectations as to how and when correction should be offered will vary. Many teachers have difficulty finding the optimal amount of correction—enough to focus students on monitoring errors, but not so much as to demoralize or discourage them. It is important to target specific types of errors when correcting students, rather than aiming to correct everything they say or write. The focus of the current lesson and your knowledge of your students' strengths and weaknesses will dictate whether you focus on form, pronunciation, meaning, or appropriate use. Discuss error correction with your students and determine how they would like to be corrected. Aim to combine or vary your correction techniques depending on the focus of the lesson and the needs of your students.

Spoken Errors

There are a variety of ways to correct spoken errors. If a student makes an error repeatedly, stop him or her and encourage self-correction by repeating the error with a questioning (rising) tone, or by gesturing. Develop a set of gestures that you use consistently so students know exactly what you are pointing out. For example, problems with the past tense can be indicated by pointing backwards over your shoulder, future time can be indicated by pointing your hand ahead of you, and third person can be shown by holding up three fingers. (Be careful not to choose gestures that are considered offensive by some cultures.) If your students feel comfortable being corrected by their peers, encourage them to help each other when they hear mistakes. Another option is to keep track of spoken errors during an activity, and then at the end elicit corrections from the class by writing the incorrect sentences you heard on the board. This way, students are not singled out for their mistakes, but get the feedback they need.

Written Errors

It is important to encourage students to monitor their written errors and learn strategies to self-correct their writing. Establish a standard set of symbols to use when marking students' work. For example, *pl* for plural, *agr* for agreement, *s* for subject, *v* for verb. When you find an error, do not correct it, but instead mark it with a symbol. Students will have to work out the exact nature of their error and correct it themselves. This will reduce your correction time and encourage students to learn for themselves by reflecting on their errors. Peer correction is another useful technique by which students can provide feedback on a partner's work. In order for it to be effective, give students clear and limited objectives and do not expect them to identify all the errors in their classmate's work. Note that students may be resistant to peer correction at first, and nervous about learning others' mistakes. But once they develop a trust in one another, they will be surprised at how much they can learn from their classmates.

Tour of a Student Book Chapter

Each chapter in *Grammar Sense 4* follows this format:

The **Grammar in Discourse** section introduces the target structure in its natural context via a high-interest authentic reading text.

Authentic reading texts show how language is really used.

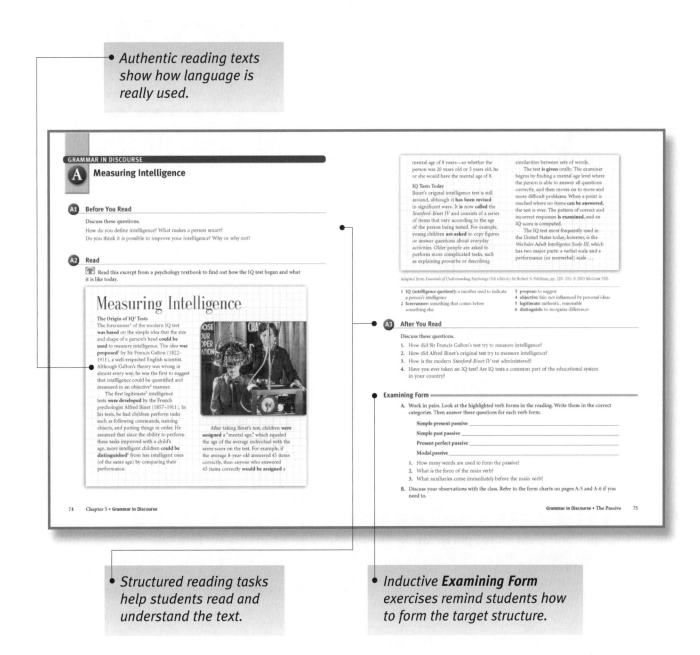

Structured reading tasks help students read and understand the text.

*Inductive **Examining Form** exercises remind students how to form the target structure.*

The **Form, Meaning, and Use** section(s) offers clear presentation of the target structure, detailed notes, and comprehensive explanations of how the target structure is used, and exercises to practice using it appropriately.

• Inductive *Examining Meaning and Use* exercises encourage students to analyze how we use the target structure.

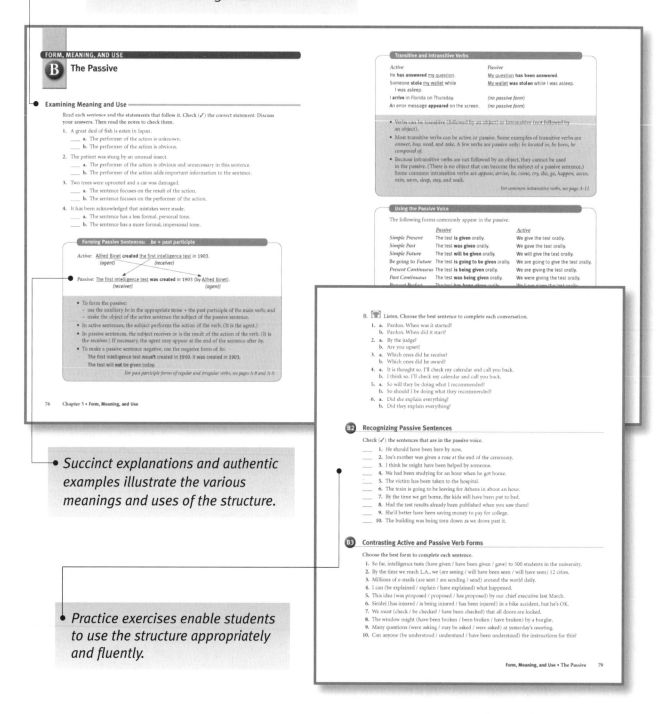

• Succinct explanations and authentic examples illustrate the various meanings and uses of the structure.

• Practice exercises enable students to use the structure appropriately and fluently.

The **Writing** section guides students through the process of applying their grammatical knowledge to academic writing.

Editing *sections train students to recognize and avoid common errors.*

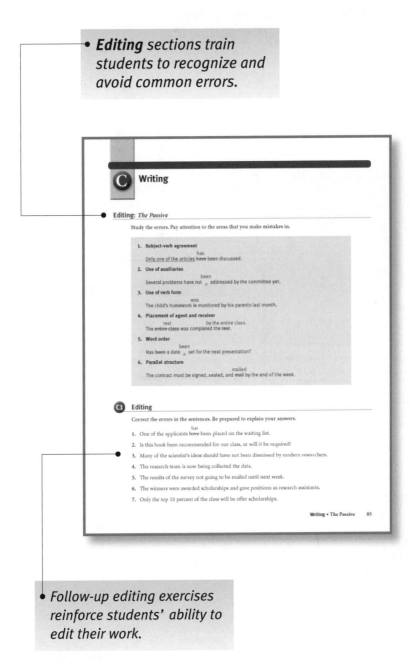

C Writing

Editing: *The Passive*

Study the errors. Pay attention to the areas that you make mistakes in.

> 1. **Subject-verb agreement**
>   has
>   Only one of the articles have been discussed.
>
> 2. **Use of auxiliaries**
>   been
>   Several problems have not ∧ addressed by the committee yet.
>
> 3. **Use of verb form**
>   was
>   The child's homework is monitored by his parents last month.
>
> 4. **Placement of agent and receiver**
>   test   by the entire class.
>   The entire class was completed the test.
>
> 5. **Word order**
>   been
>   Has been a date ∧ set for the next presentation?
>
> 6. **Parallel structure**
>   mailed
>   The contract must be signed, sealed, and mail by the end of the week.

C1 Editing

Correct the errors in the sentences. Be prepared to explain your answers.

  has
1. One of the applicants have been placed on the waiting list.

2. Is this book been recommended for our class, or will it be required?

3. Many of the scientist's ideas should have not been dismissed by modern researchers.

4. The research team is now being collected the data.

5. The results of the survey not going to be mailed until next week.

6. The winners were awarded scholarships and gave positions as research assistants.

7. Only the top 10 percent of the class will be offer scholarships.

Writing • The Passive 85

Follow-up editing exercises reinforce students' ability to edit their work.

The **Writing** section provides opportunities for analyzing target structures in the context of model passages, and then constructing a grammatically accurate and appropriate essay.

*Expanded **Beyond the Sentence** sections show how structures function together in extended discourse.*

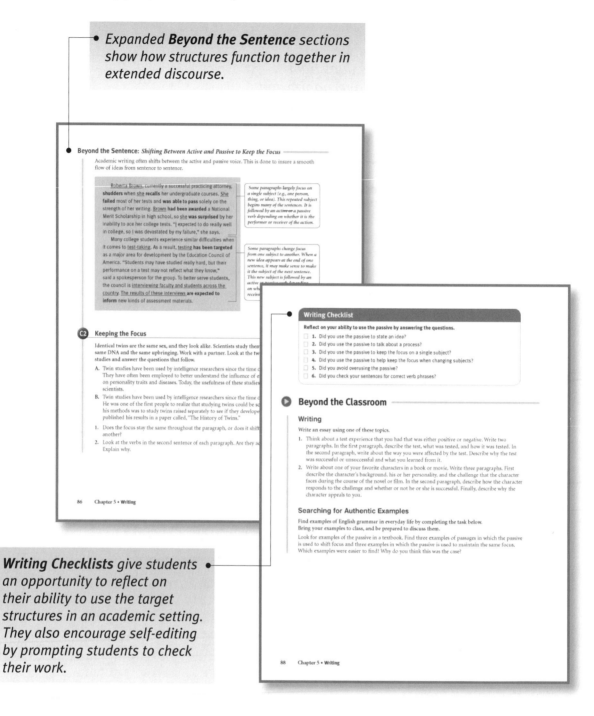

***Writing Checklists** give students an opportunity to reflect on their ability to use the target structures in an academic setting. They also encourage self-editing by prompting students to check their work.*

Special Sections appear throughout the chapters, with clear explanations, authentic examples, and follow-up exercises.

Vocabulary Notes *highlight the important connection between key vocabulary and grammatical structures.*

Writing Tips *help students understand why certain grammatical structures have a practical application in academic writing.*

Usage Notes *offer extended structure-specific information and additional practice for students.*

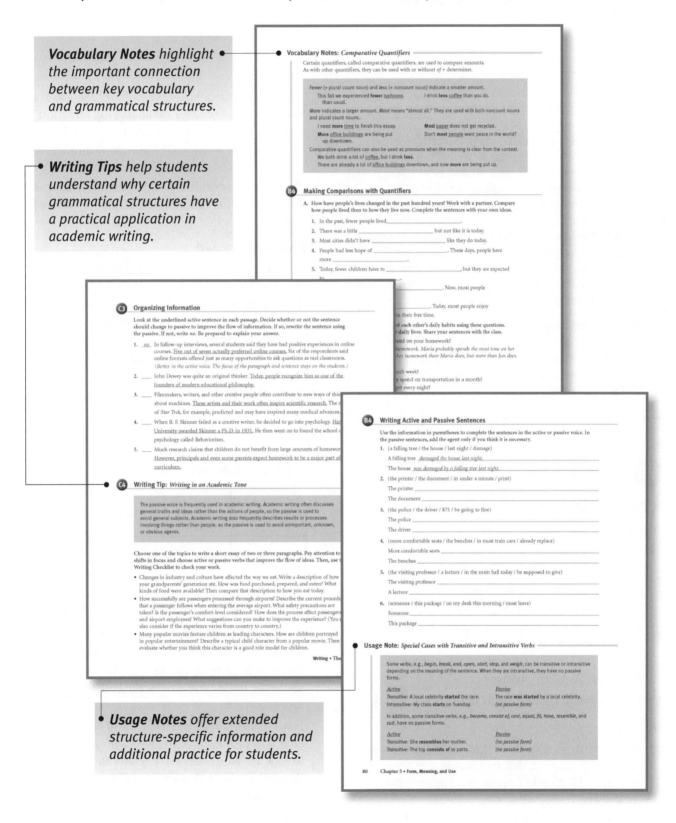

1

The Present

Overview

The simple present is used to describe actions or states that have a general, habitual, and unchanging sense. The present continuous is used to describe events that are in progress now or over a period of time. The present perfect is used to describe activities and states completed at an indefinite time in the past, or for activities and states beginning in the past and continuing in the present. Finally, the present perfect continuous is used to describe activities beginning in the past and continuing in the present, or activities that were in progress but have just ended.

Form: Students may shift inappropriately between similar present tenses, such as between the simple present and present continuous. Draw students' attention to the use of *be* with the continuous but not with the simple present.

A GRAMMAR IN DISCOURSE

Changes in Language Learning

A1: Before You Read

- Write *globalization* on the board and discuss the meaning as a class. Ask students *How is globalization changing language learning?*

- Have students work in small groups to discuss the questions. Ask each group to make a list of the most popular foreign languages to study in their countries. Then ask students to list reasons why those languages are studied.

- Discuss the lists that students have created as a class.

A2: Read

- Ask students to scan the article. Have them focus on the title, subtitle, first paragraph, and final paragraph. Tell them to note quickly any unknown vocabulary.

- After students have scanned the article, ask them what they think it is about.

- Have students read for detail, paying attention to unknown vocabulary. Remind them to infer the meaning of a word from the context and to use the glossary only as a way to check themselves.

- Review new vocabulary with students as necessary. Elicit how other students established meaning from context.

A3: After You Read

- Read the first question aloud. Ask *What does the word* trend *refer to?* (It refers to the fact that more American students are beginning to study Chinese.) Have students write a short response to the question. Discuss as a class.

- Read the second question aloud and discuss as a class.

EXAMINING FORM

- Have students examine the highlighted words in the article. Ask them to identify the verb forms.

- As students work through the article, write the following chart on the board:

Simple Present	Present Continuous	Present Perfect	Present Perfect Continuous

- Have students add the verb forms they found in the article on the board. Correct as necessary. Ask the two questions from number 1 *What do you notice about the main verb? Is it in the base form, or is there an ending?*

- Have students read question 2 and circle the auxiliaries for each of the tenses. Prompt students to identify which auxiliary relates to which tense. Remind students that they should only note auxiliaries that occur before the main verb.

- Tell students to compare answers in pairs. Then discuss their answers as a class.

- To reinforce the differences between simple and continuous tenses, have students work again in pairs. Student A will read a sample simple present sentence from the chart, and Student B will repeat the sentence with the verb in the continuous tense. Have students exchange roles. Then ask students to contrast the present perfect and present perfect continuous forms in the same way.

Trouble Spots

Stative verbs (*know, believe, have*, etc.) do not typically occur in continuous tenses because they express unchanging states or conditions. However, avoid telling students that stative verbs can never be used in the continuous form or that they only appear in the simple present. There are times (as students will see later in this chapter) when we use stative verbs to stress emotion (e.g., I'm just loving this book!). In addition, some stative verbs can have active meanings as well (e.g., *I'm tasting the soup to see if it's too hot.*). In both of these cases, the present continuous is used.

B) FORM, MEANING, AND USE

The Present

EXAMINING MEANING AND USE

- Have students work in pairs to answer the questions (1. a; 2. b; 3. b; 4. a).
- Give students a few minutes to refer to the Notes to check their answers.
- Call on students to read the questions and answer aloud. Discuss any disagreements and have students make any necessary corrections.

Simple Present

- Have students read the Notes. Ask *What are the three main uses of the simple present?* Write these in a simple chart on the board like below:

Habits and repeated activities	Facts and general truths	States or conditions

- Ask students to work in pairs to list example sentences for each of the simple present uses (e.g., *I check my e-mail every morning* under *Habits and Repeated Activities*).

- Have a few students write their examples in the chart on the board. Discuss as a class.

Present Continuous

- Have students read the Notes. On the board, write *Activities in Progress Now or Over a Period of Time.* Then below that, write *Time Expressions.*
- As a class, brainstorm time expressions that can be used with the present continuous. Write these on the board. Allow for correction if inappropriate time expressions are given.
- Ask students to write new example sentences for the Notes using the time expressions listed on the board. Tell students that these sentences should be for activities in progress now or over a period of time.
- Share sentences as a class.

Present Perfect

- Have students read the Notes. Reinforce the information by asking students to match the example sentences to the bulleted explanations.
- Circulate and help students stay focused. Check that they understand the explanations by asking *How does the example sentence illustrate the explanation?* Discuss answers as a class.

Present Perfect Continuous

- Have students close their books. Tell students that you are going to read sentences to them and that they should think about whether the action is continuing or completed.
- Read aloud the three sentences from the Notes. After each sentence, ask *What is the action in this sentence? Is the action completed or is it continuing?* Ask students to qualify their answers. If necessary, write the sentences on the board.
- Ask students to open their books and read the bulleted explanations.

Comparing Present Perfect and Present Perfect Continuous

- Ask students to read the first examples under *Different Meanings.* Ask students, *How are these two sentences different?* Then ask how the verb endings in each sentence are different (the completed action ends in *–ed*, and the continuing action ends in *–ing*).
- Now have students read the sentences under *Similar Meanings.* In pairs, ask students to write new examples with the verbs *live, teach, sleep, study,* and *work.* Remind students that they will write two sentences for each verb: one with the present perfect and the other with the present perfect continuous.

- Circulate and monitor. Encourage students to write pairs of sentences with similar meanings, like the ones in the Notes.
- Then ask students to share their sentences and discuss as a class.

C WRITING

Editing: *The Present*

- Have students close their books. Tell them you will write incorrect sentences on the board and then call on students to correct them.
- Write the first example on the board but without the correction (* *The publishers of the new software is planning to market it internationally.*) Call on a student to correct the sentence (change *is* to *are*). Assist as necessary. Then ask the student to explain his or her correction and describe the error.
- Repeat as above with the rest of the examples. Then have students open their books and read the Editing box. Discuss as necessary.

Beyond the Sentence: *Describing Current Situations*

- Have students read the passage and identify the main idea (that almost everyone in the United States is familiar with Chinese food).
- Ask students why the writer chose the simple present for the thesis statement (because it establishes a present context by making a general statement about a current situation). Draw attention to the first call-out box. Then direct students to examine the second call-out box on the left and call on a student to read aloud the correlating sentence.
- Ask students to give possible reasons why the writer chose the present and present perfect continuous near the end of the paragraph (to show that the situation is changing). Discuss as a class.

Vocabulary Notes: *Time Expressions*

- In pairs, have students give spoken examples to each other with each time expression and all the corresponding verb forms. For example, they can give an example sentence with *nowadays* in sentences with the simple present or present continuous.

ADDITIONAL ACTIVITIES

The purpose of the activity is to provide practice using all the present tenses in an authentic situation.

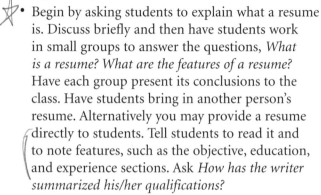

- Begin by asking students to explain what a resume is. Discuss briefly and then have students work in small groups to answer the questions, *What is a resume? What are the features of a resume?* Have each group present its conclusions to the class. Have students bring in another person's resume. Alternatively you may provide a resume directly to students. Tell students to read it and to note features, such as the objective, education, and experience sections. Ask *How has the writer summarized his/her qualifications?*
- Have students individually paraphrase the information from these sections in paragraph form. Explain that the summary should be written using present tenses as much as possible. Have students trade their summaries (but not their resumes) with another student for peer-editing. Remind students to use the Writing Checklist on page 14. Tell students that they are to edit the summary and make suggestions for revising.

2 The Past

Overview

The simple past is used to describe actions completed at a specific time in the past, while the past continuous is used to describe an activity in progress at a specific time in the past. These two tenses often occur in the same sentence to show a continuing action (in the past continuous) that was interrupted by a transitory action (in the simple past). The present perfect is used to refer to an unspecified time in the past. Students often confuse the present perfect with the simple past. The past perfect is also a candidate for confusion. The past perfect is used to indicate the earlier of two past events. The past perfect continuous indicates an event in progress before a previous time in the past.

Form: The major challenge of the past tenses is to distinguish between the simple past and past participle forms of irregular verbs. Before you begin:

- review the opening page of this chapter and then brainstorm what the students observe or remember about these verb forms.
- review key terms from this chapter, such as *tense shifting*, *clause*, *narrative*, *time expressions*, *flashbacks*, and *subject-verb agreement*.

A GRAMMAR IN DISCOURSE

Ripening at the Center of the World

A1: Before You Read

- Have students work in small groups to discuss the questions.
- Call on students to share their answers with the class.
- Write the word *Brazil* on the board. Ask students to respond by suggested words they associate with *Brazil*. Allow students to respond freely and note keywords on the board.

A2: Read

- On the board, write *Ripening at the Center of the World*. Ask students to guess the meaning of the

title and to predict the subject of the essay.

- Have students read the essay. Ask if their predictions were correct.
- Divide students into small groups and assign each group a paragraph from the essay. Ask each group to write a one- or two-sentence summary of the assigned paragraph.
- Now put students into new groups so each new group has a person to summarize each paragraph. Each member will summarize his or her paragraph and answer any questions.

A3: After You Read

- Have students do the exercise and mark the places in the essay where they found their answers.
- Ask students to compare answers with a partner.
- Circulate and note any problematic areas. Discuss these as a class.

EXAMINING FORM

- On the board, write the sentences: *Last night at 6:00, I ate dinner* and *An art exhibit opened in town yesterday*. Ask students to read the sentences silently. Underline the verbs in the sentences (*ate* and *opened*). Ask students to identify how these two verbs are different (*ate* is irregular and *opened* is regular).
- Write the following chart on the board:

Simple Past	Past Continuous	Past Perfect	Past Perfect Continuous

- Have students copy the chart. In pairs, ask students to fill in the chart with verb forms from the reading.

- Ask one student to complete each column of the chart on the board. As a class, suggest additions and make any necessary corrections.
- Answer questions as a class. Discuss any disagreements and have students make necessary corrections.

Trouble Spots
If students have trouble understanding the perfect and continuous forms, it may be useful to explain that in linguistic terms, perfect and continuous forms are called aspects. This means that they do not denote time so much as they are concerned with such notions as continuation and completion.

B) FORM, MEANING, AND USE 1

Simple Past and the Past Continuous

EXAMINING MEANING AND USE
- Have students work in pairs to answer the questions (1. b; 2. b; 3. b; 4. a).
- Give students a few minutes to refer to the Notes to check their answers.
- Call on students to read the questions and answer aloud. Discuss any disagreements and have students make any necessary corrections.

Trouble Spots
Students often confuse the simple past and present perfect. Remind them that the simple past is used for completed past actions, often with a time reference. The present perfect refers to the past without a specific time reference. One way to assist students is by providing example sentences that use the present perfect but require the simple past to establish time.

Simple Past
- Ask students to read the Notes. In pairs, have students discuss how they know from each sentence that the activity or state was completed in the past (from the time expressions and the use of the simple past).

Past Continuous
- Have students close their books. Tell students you are going to read sentences to them. They should think about the actions for each sentence.
- Read aloud the first example sentence from the Notes. Ask students to listen again and list the actions occurring in the sentence in sequence.

(First she was filling out an application. Then the computer crashed.) Read the sentence aloud again if necessary. Repeat for the next example sentence.
- Ask students to open their books and read the bulleted explanations.

Comparing Simple Past and Past Continuous
- Have students read the Notes. Reinforce the information by asking students to match the example sentences to the bulleted explanations.
- Circulate and help students keep focused. Check that they understand the explanations by asking *How do we know this action was (or was not) completed?*

Comparing Simple Past and Present Perfect
- Have students read the Notes. Ask students to brainstorm situations where the simple past and present perfect are used differently and discuss as a class.

C) FORM, MEANING, AND USE 2

Past Perfect and Past Perfect Continuous

EXAMINING MEANING AND USE
- Have students work in pairs to answer the questions (1. a, b; 2. b, a; 3. b, a).
- Give students a few minutes to refer to the Notes to check their answers.
- Call on students to read the questions and answer aloud. Discuss any disagreements and have students make any necessary corrections.

Past Perfect
- Ask students to read the Notes. Then have students write new example sentences in the past perfect. Circulate and monitor.
- Call on several students to write their sentences on the board. As students write, ask the rest of the class if the sentences are correct.

Past Perfect Continuous
- Have students close their books. Tell students you are going to read sentences to them. Tell them while they listen, they should think about the actions in each sentence.
- Read aloud the first example sentence. Ask students what the actions are in the sentence (*had been traveling, broke down*). Ask *Which is the earlier action and which is the later?*

- Then ask students *How long had he been traveling?* Repeat for the next example sentence.
- Ask students to open their books and read the bulleted explanation.

Comparing Past Perfect and Past Perfect Continuous

- Have students close their books. Write the following pairs of sentences on the board *When I met her, she had written the novel. When I met her, she had been writing the novel. When I got home he had made dinner. When I got home he had been making dinner.*
- As a class, discuss which sentences indicate that the action is finished (the first in each pair) and which indicate that the action is not finished.

Comparing Simple Past and Past Perfect

- Ask students to read the Notes. Then have students write new example sentences in the simple past and past perfect. Tell students to include information from the bulleted explanations with each example.
- Call on several students to write their sentences on the board. As students write, ask the rest of the class if the sentences are correct.

D WRITING

Editing: *The Past*

- Read through the Editing box as a class. After each example sentence, call on a student to explain why the sentence was corrected as it was. Discuss any questions as necessary.
- Have students work in pairs to write new example sentences for each error type. Explain that they will write sentences with errors and corrections. Circulate and assist students as necessary.
- Ask for one volunteer for each error type to write his or her sentence on the board. Ask the student to describe the error and explain how he or she corrected it. Discuss as a class.

Beyond the Sentence: *Shifting Between Past and Present*

- Have students read the passage. Ask students to read through each call-out box and mark whether it refers to a past or present verb form. Ask students for their general impressions of when past and present verb forms were used in the passage.
- Tell students to work in pairs to create a list of reasons why the past or present forms were used

in the places marked in the passage. Circulate and make sure that students are referring to the call-out boxes for each verb form.
- As a class, go through each highlighted verb form in the passage. Call on students to give reasons why the verb form was used.

ADDITIONAL ACTIVITIES

This activity is intended to give students additional exposure to the relationship between the simple past and the past perfect and to build extended writing skills.

- Refer students to exercise C3 on page 26. As in that exercise, students will be using the past tenses from this chapter to describe flashbacks of background information. Each composition should be at least two paragraphs. Write the following guidelines on the board: 1. The introduction should use the simple past or past continuous; 2. Background material should be expressed in the past perfect; 3. Concluding sentences should use the simple past or past continuous.
- Provide a model on the board: *On my way home from the airport after a perfect vacation, I was stuck in heavy city traffic. My car was barely moving at all. To make matters worse, it was snowing heavily and the roads were slippery. As I looked around, I could feel my mellow vacation mood disappearing. After ten minutes, then twenty, my mind began to wander. Only 24 hours before I had been . . .*
- As a class, brainstorm possible flashbacks. Tell students that they may begin writing when ready. Circulate as necessary and assist students in developing a situation for a flashback. Remind students that they will need to use the appropriate tenses. Refer students to the Form, Meaning, and use Notes in the chapter as needed (pages 18–19 and 23–24).
- Share selected stories with the whole class.

3

THE FUTURE

Overview

This chapter presents the use of future forms that refer to specific points in the future or show relationships between two future situations. Since many future forms may be used in place of one another and the choice of form must be established by context, it will be helpful to students to learn how to differentiate between situations where the choice of form is clear. Students must learn how to choose the future form that best suits their intended meaning.

Form: Students may have difficulty distinguishing the uses of the future continuous and future perfect continuous, as well as knowing how to use combinations of the continuous and perfect forms. Before you begin, review key terms from this chapter, such as *prediction*, *time clause*, *stative meaning*, *auxiliary verb*, *parallel form*, and *word order*.

A) GRAMMAR IN DISCOURSE

The Secret Treasures of Zeugma

A1: Before You Read

*   Ask students to read the information and note any unfamiliar vocabulary. Ask students *What is Zeugma? What happened there?* Then answer any vocabulary questions (e.g., about the words *Roman Empire*, *artifacts*, *Euphrates*, *archaeologists*).
*   Have students work in small groups to discuss the Before You Read questions.
*   Call on students to share their answers with the class.

A2: Read

*   Ask students to scan the excerpts. Have them focus on the format of the excerpts and the headings. Then have students give their impressions.
*   Next have students read the excerpt to find out what archaeologists did to save artifacts from Zeugma.
*   Have students work in small groups to discuss the question and to list what archaeologists saved before

the flooding. Ask *Do you think the dam or the ruins are more valuable? Why?* Discuss as a class.

A3: After You Read

*   Have students do the exercise individually and mark the places in the reading where they found their answers.
*   Ask students to compare answers with a partner.
*   Circulate and note any problematic items. Discuss these as a class.

EXAMINING FORM

*   Have students examine the highlighted words in the reading and then write them in the correct categories.
*   Ask students to work in pairs to answer the three questions. Circulate and monitor. As students finish, combine pairs into small groups. Have students compare answers.
*   Call on groups to share their answers with the class. Discuss and allow correction when necessary.

B) FORM, MEANING, AND USE

The Future

EXAMINING MEANING AND USE

*   Have students work in pairs to answer the questions (1. a; 2. a; 3. b).
*   Give students a few minutes to refer to the Notes to check their answers.
*   Call on students to read the questions and answers aloud. Discuss any disagreements and have students make any necessary corrections.

Overview: *Basic Future Forms*

- Have students read the Notes. Put students into five groups and assign each group one of the future forms from the Notes. Tell each group they will present a brief overview to the class.

- Circulate and monitor. Remind students to include any relative information about time clauses and adverbs.

- Have each group present their assigned form. Discuss as a class.

Plans vs. Quick Decisions

- Have students read the Notes. On the board write the column headings *Planned Future Activities* and *Quick Decisions*.

- Ask students to write new example sentences with future forms for expressing plans. Circulate and monitor.

- Call on several students to write their sentences on the board. As students write, ask the rest of the class if the sentences are correct.

More Definite Plans and Scheduled Events

- Have students close their books. Tell students that you are going to read sentences to them. Tell them while they listen, they should think about whether the activity is planned or scheduled.

- Read aloud the first example sentence. Ask students *Is this activity planned in advance or a quick decision? How do you know?* Read the sentence aloud again if necessary. Repeat for the rest of the example sentences.

- Ask students to open their books and read the bulleted explanations. Answer any questions and discuss as a class.

Predictions and Expectations

- Have students read the Notes. In pairs, have students write new example sentences for each bulleted explanation.

- Call on several students to write their sentences on the board. As students write, ask the rest of the class if the sentences are correct. Discuss as needed.

Future Perfect and Future Perfect Continuous

- Have students read the Notes. Reinforce the information by asking students to match the example sentences to the bulleted explanations.

- Circulate and help students keep focused. Check that they understand the explanations and provide assistance as needed.

C) WRITING

Editing: *The Future*

- Before beginning, review the terms *parallel form* and *sentence fragments*. Explain and discuss these types of errors as a class.

- Read through the Editing box as a class. After each example sentence, call on a student to explain why the sentence was corrected as it was. Discuss any questions as necessary.

Beyond the Sentence: *Shifting Between the Past, Present, and Future*

- Have students read the passage. Ask students to identify the main point of the passage (that homeowners in Houston are working to preserve historic homes in their neighborhood). Briefly discuss as a class.

- Draw students' attention to the first call-out box on the left. Ask students *Is this sentence transitioning from the past or future? What is the event that is not resolved?*

- Have students read the next sentence. Ask students to identify the verb forms used in this sentence. Then direct students to read the next call-out box.

- Have students read the remaining call-out boxes. Ask students whether time expressions were used when shifting to future time or past time. Discuss as a class.

Vocabulary Notes: *Future Time Expressions*

- Have students read through the information in the Vocabulary Notes. Ask students to brainstorm a short list of time expressions. As a class, come up with example sentences that refer to plans at a specific time and then plans at an indefinite time.

- Call on students to share their sentences. Allow students to correct and discuss the differences between specific time and indefinite time.

- Tell students to complete the exercise. Circulate and monitor as necessary. Discuss answers as a class.

The purpose of this activity is to have students discern appropriate uses of future forms and build skills in shifting between these forms within a paragraph.

- Either provide students with a copy of a week-long travel schedule, or ask them to bring one to class (travel brochures are a good place to look). Ask students to write a paragraph describing the activities on the schedule. Tell students that they should use *will*, be going to, the simple present and the present continuous. Refer students to the Form, Meaning, and Use Notes in the chapter as needed (pages 37–39).

- Ask students to share their drafts with a partner for editing, utilizing the Writing Checklist. Monitor students as they edit. Be sure to check for proper control of future forms and time expressions.

4 MODALS

Overview

Modals are auxiliary verbs that are used to express advice, necessity, prohibition, lack of necessity, obligation, or degrees of possibility. Students should be familiar with auxiliaries and word order. This chapter is a good opportunity to focus on writing.

Form: The key challenges are remembering
- when to use *to* before the main verb (*have to, ought to*).
- that past modals are formed with *have* + past participle.

A GRAMMAR IN DISCOURSE

Astrology and Psychology

A1: Before You Read

- Write the word *astrology* on the board and discuss the meaning as a class. Then ask students *What is a horoscope? How many of you read your horoscope?*

- Write the word *psychology* on the board. Elicit a variety of definitions and ask students how astrology might relate to psychology. Discuss briefly as a class.

- Have students work in small groups to discuss the Before You Read questions. Remind them to keep in mind the definitions of psychology and astrology that they just discussed.

- Call on students to share their answers with the class.

A2: Read

- Ask students to scan the article. Have them focus on the title, the first two sentences of each paragraph, and the conclusion. Tell them quickly to note any unknown vocabulary.

- After students have scanned the article, ask them to predict what researchers are learning about astrology and psychology.

- Have students read for detail, paying attention to unknown vocabulary. Remind them to infer the meaning of a word from the context and to use the glossary only as a way to check themselves.

- Discuss the article as a class.

A3: After You Read

- Have students do the exercise in pairs and mark the places in the reading where they found their answers.

- Ask students to compare answers with another pair.

- As a class, discuss the questions. Focus on the second questions in the first and second items. Ask students *How does psychology relate to astrology?*

- As an additional activity, bring in a horoscope from a magazine or newspaper. Ask students to consider the information in the horoscope and then share their opinions.

EXAMINING FORM

- Have students work in pairs and examine the highlighted verb forms in the article. Tell students to think about why these words were highlighted and how they might relate to one another.

- As students work, write the following chart on the board:

Simple Modal	Continuous Modal	Past Modal

- Have students add the verb forms they found in the article on the board. Discuss and correct as necessary.

- Ask students to answer the three questions in order to understand the form of modals and the verbs that follow them.

Modals of Advice, Necessity, Prohibition, and Obligation

EXAMINING MEANING AND USE

- Have students work in pairs to answer the questions (1. a; 2. b; 3. a; 4. b).

- Give students a few minutes to refer to the Notes to check their answers.

- Call on students to read the questions and answer aloud. Discuss any disagreements and have students make any necessary corrections.

Modals of Advice

- Have students read the Notes. Reinforce the information by asking students to match the example sentences to the bulleted explanations.

- Circulate and help students stay focused. Check that they understand the explanations by asking *How does the example sentence illustrate the explanation?* Discuss as a class.

Modals of Necessity

- Ask students to read the Notes. In pairs, have students write new example sentences.

- Write the following chart on the board:

Present/Future Necessity	Past Necessity

- Call on several students to write their sentences on the board. As students write, ask the class if the sentences are correct. Discuss as needed.

Modals of Prohibition and Lack of Necessity

- Have students read the Notes. Put students into groups of three or four. Assign each group one of the four forms presented in the Notes. Tell students to prepare a short summary of each form to present to the class.

- Circulate and monitor. Assist students in summarizing the information as necessary.

- Call on each group to present their summary to the class. Prompt students to ask questions and assist.

Modals of Obligation

- Have students close their books. Tell students you are going to read sentences to them. Tell them while they listen, they should think about whether the sentence refers to actions in the present/future or past.

- Read aloud the first example sentence. Ask students *What does the modal in this sentence suggest?* (obligation) Then ask students if it refers to a present/future obligation or past obligation. Read the sentence aloud again if necessary. Repeat for the rest of the example sentences.

- Ask students to open their books and read the bulleted explanations. Answer any questions and discuss as a class.

Modals of Possibility

EXAMINING MEANING AND USE

- Have students work in pairs to answer the questions (b, a, c).

- Give students a few minutes to refer to the Notes to check their answers.

- Call on students to read the questions and answer aloud. Discuss any disagreements and have students make any necessary corrections.

Modals of Possibility

- Have students close their books. Tell students that you are going to read sentences to them. Tell them while they listen, they should think about the meaning of the sentence and the modal it uses.

- Read aloud the first example sentence. Then ask *What modals were used? What do these modals mean?* Read the sentence aloud again if necessary. Repeat for the rest of the example sentences.

- Ask students to open their books and read the bulleted explanations. Answer any questions and discuss as a class.

Weaker Certainty

- Have students read the Notes. Reinforce the information by asking *What is certainty?* Discuss the term as a class and ask students to compare it with the term *possibility*.

- Write these modals on the board: *could, might (not),* and *may (not).* Ask students to work in pairs to write sentences with these modals as examples of weaker certainty. Circulate and monitor.

- Call on several students to share their sentences. As a class, discuss whether or not the sentences express weaker certainty.

Assumptions

- Ask students to read the Notes. Then have students write new example sentences that make assumptions in the present/future and past.

- Have students exchange sentences with a partner. Tell students to read their partner's sentences and to state what assumption is being made in each sentence. Circulate and monitor.

- As a class, discuss what assumptions were made by their partner and which modals were used. If necessary, ask students to clarify differences between assumptions, certainty, and possibility by having them arrange the terms from week to strong (possibility ⟶ assumption ⟶ certainty and impossibility).

Strong Certainty

- Have students read the Notes. Reinforce the information by asking students to match example sentences to the bulleted explanations.

- Circulate and help students keep focused. Check that they understand the explanations by asking *Which modal is typically used to express strong certainty about the future?* Discuss answers.

Impossibility

- Write the first example from the Notes on the board. Ask a student to identify the modal + verb in the example *(couldn't be)*. Then ask *Is it possible that the speaker could be more pleased?*

- Write the second example from the Notes on the board. Ask a student to identify the modal + verb in the example *(can't have been)*. Then ask *How is the verb form in this sentence different from the previous one?* (This sentence refers to the past.)

- Tell students to open their books and read the Notes. Discuss as necessary.

D) WRITING

Editing: *Modals*

- Have students close their books. Tell them you will write incorrect sentences on the board and then call on students to correct them.

- Write the first example on the board but without the correction (* *Non-citizens may not to serve on a jury*). Call on a student to correct the sentence (remove *to*). Assist as necessary. Then ask the student to explain the correction and the error.

- Repeat as above with the next five examples. Then have students open their books and read the Editing box. Discuss as needed.

Beyond the Sentence: *Reacting to Situations with Advice, Guesses, and Conclusions*

- Have students read the passage and identify the thesis statement (that most children have been bullied at school). Briefly discuss as a class.

- Direct students to read the first call-out box. Ask students what possible situation the writer is describing (that bullies might be better and stronger than their peers). Then ask students to identify which modal has been used *(might)*. Now tell students to read through the first paragraph and note any alternatives to this situation. Discuss as a class.

- Have students read the second call-out box. To check that students understand the meaning, call on a couple of students to note what guesses or conclusions were made and the modals that were used.

- Now direct students to the call-out box on the right. Ask *What advice or suggestions are given here? What modal did the writer use?*

- Have students read the final call-out box and the last paragraph. Ask students to note what predictions the writer makes. Discuss as necessary.

Vocabulary Notes: *Adverbs*

- Divide students into three groups to brainstorm situations where they might use these adverbs.

- Then have each group write one short (2–4 line) skit. Assign as follows:
  1. A skit in which an adverb is used to weaken advice
  2. A skit in which an adverb is used to strengthen advice
  3. A skit in which an adverb is used to replace a modal of possibility or certainty.

- Have the groups perform their skits. Ask the class to pick out which adverb was used to weaken or strengthen advice, or as a substitute for a modal.

ADDITIONAL ACTIVITIES

This activity provides students with engaging writing and speaking practice with modals. If possible, consider bringing in an advice column from a local newspaper to share with students before beginning.

- Ask students if they are familiar with advice columns typically found in newspapers and some magazines. Call on students to elicit what they know about advice columns. Tell them that they will be working with a partner to write a short letter stating a problem and then writing an appropriate advice column. Tell students that they should focus on using the modals from the chapter.

- Before students begin, brainstorm some typical and appropriate problems that might be found in an advice column. List these on the board, and provide additional examples only when necessary. Call on a few students to give some general advice on one or two of the problems. Prompt students to use modals.

- Have students work in pairs to write a letter to a newspaper advice column. Refer students to the Form, Meaning, and Use Notes in the chapter as needed (pages 54—56 and 62-63).

- Ask for volunteers to read their letters to the class. Briefly allow students to respond to the letter by suggesting the advice that they would give.

- Have students complete the exercise by writing a response to the letter as a short advice column. Make sure students work collaboratively and correct students as needed.

- Have each pair give a brief summary of the problem in the letter to the advice column and then read aloud the advice column response. Discuss any disagreements about the advice given as needed and prompt students to use appropriate modals.

5

The Passive

Overview

The passive is a form in which more importance is given to the receiver (or object) of an action than to the performer (or agent) of that action. In the passive, the position of the subject and object within a clause are reversed; the auxiliary *be* is added and indicates tense and agreement; and the main verb is in the form of a past participle. The performer of the action is retained only if known or important to the context and is preceded by the particle *by*. The use of the passive is a convention in scientific and some other types of academic writing.

Form: The passive is limited to transitive verbs including transitive phrasal verbs (e.g., *The train was held up by Jesse James.*). The passive occurs in all tenses as well as with modals.

A GRAMMAR IN DISCOURSE

Measuring Intelligence

A1: Before You Read

- Ask students if they are familiar with IQ tests. Ask if any students have ever taken one. Allow students time to share, but limit students to talking about the test and their impressions.

- Have students work in small groups to discuss the Before You Read questions. Ask students to make a short list of ways to measure intelligence. Circulate and monitor and keep students focused.

- Discuss as a class. Call on students to share their answers.

- As a follow-up to the last question, ask students to talk about specific ways to improve intelligence.

A2: Read

- Ask students to scan the excerpt. Have them focus on the title, subtitle, first paragraph, and final paragraph. Tell them quickly to note any unknown vocabulary.

- After students have scanned the excerpt, ask them what they think it is about.

- Have students read for detail, paying attention to unknown vocabulary. Remind them to infer the meaning of a word from the context and to use the glossary only as a way to check themselves.

- Review new vocabulary with students as necessary. Elicit how students established meaning from context.

A3: After You Read

- Have students do the exercise in pairs and mark the places in the reading where they found their answers.

- Ask students to compare answers with another pair.

- Circulate and note any problematic items.

- As a follow-up activity, ask students to think about the characteristics of an intelligent person. Discuss how the way people view intelligence has changed.

EXAMINING FORM

- Have students examine the highlighted words in the reading. On the board, write *Passive* and call on a student to provide an example of a passive form from the reading.

- Write the sentence that this verb came from. Next to this sentence, write *Active* and then rewrite the sentence in the active voice. Ask students *How are these two forms similar? How are they different?*

- Direct students to work in pairs to do the exercise. Circulate and monitor. As students finish, combine pairs into small groups. Compare answers.

- Write the following chart on the board:

Simple Present Passive	Simple Past Passive	Present Perfect Passive	Modal Passive

- Have students add the verb forms they found in the reading on the board. Correct as necessary.

The Passive

EXAMINING MEANING AND USE

- Have students work in pairs to answer the questions (1. b; 2. b; 3. a; 4. b).

- Give students a few minutes to refer to the Notes to check their answers. Make sure that they understand who the performer of the action is and what the result of the action is.

- Call on students to read the questions and answer aloud. Discuss any disagreements and have students make any necessary corrections.

Forming Passive Sentences

- Ask students to read the Notes. Then have students write new example sentences in the passive. Circulate and monitor.

- Have students exchange sentences. Ask students to first check the new example sentences and make any necessary corrections. Then instruct students to rewrite the sentences in the active.

- Write these sentences on the board *Toronto is located in Canada. My father was born in New York City.* Ask students if the sentences can be made active (No).

- As students finish the task, call on several students to write a passive and its accompanying active example on the board. Ask the class if the sentences are correct. Discuss as needed.

Transitive and Intransitive Verbs

- Have students read the Notes. Reinforce the information by asking students to match the example sentences to the bulleted explanations.

- Circulate and help students keep focused. Check that they understand the explanations by asking *How does the example sentence illustrate the explanation?* Discuss answers as a class.

Using the Passive Voice

- Ask students to read the Notes. Then, to review all of the passive forms listed in this section, place the students into five groups. Assign each group two of the passive forms. Tell students to write new example sentences in the same form as the ones they were assigned.

- As the students work, copy the chart on page 77 onto the board, leaving the *Passive* and *Active* columns empty.

- Call on someone from each group to read their new example sentences out loud. Ask the class which row the sentence belongs in (e.g. simple past, past modal) and have the student write the sentence in the appropriate row on the chart. Correct the sentence as a class.

- After all of the passive sentences have been listed and corrected, have the students work together in pairs to write corresponding active sentences for each passive. Call on students to write their active sentences in the chart. Discuss and correct as necessary.

The Agent in Passive Sentences

- Have students close their books. On the board, write the first example from the *Agent Is Not Used* and *Agent Is Used* columns. Ask students to compare the two sentences. Ask students why they think the agent is used or not used. (The first does not require an agent because it is not important. The second uses the agent to clarify meaning.)

- Write more examples of the agentless passive on the board and ask students to guess why the agent is not used.

- Ask students to open their books and read the Notes. Answer any questions and discuss as a class.

Editing: *The Passive*

- Have students close their books. Tell them you will write incorrect sentences on the board and then call on students to correct them.

- Write the first example on the board but without the correction (* *Only one of the articles have been discussed.*) Call on a student to correct the sentence (change *have* to *has*). Assist as necessary. Then ask the student to explain his or her correction and describe the error.

- Repeat as above with the rest of the examples. Then have students open their books and read the Editing box. Discuss as necessary.

Beyond the Sentence: *Shifting Between Active and Passive to Keep the Focus*

- Have students read the passage and identify the main point (that students who otherwise excel in school may not do well on tests). Briefly discuss as a class.

- Direct students to read the first sentence of the passage again, noting the highlighted words. Call on a student to identify the verbs and their subject. Ask: Is the subject the agent (the performer) or the receiver of the action? Is the sentence active or passive? Explain that when the subject is the agent, the sentence is active.

- Ask students to examine the remaining highlighted words in the first paragraph. Ask students to find the passive sentences. Ask: Is the subject the agent (the performer) or the receiver of the action? Is the sentence active or passive? Explain that when the subject is the receiver, the sentence is passive. Have students read the first call-out box. Discuss as necessary.

- To summarize the first paragraph, ask who it is about. (R. Brown). Now direct students to read the second paragraph and note the highlighted words. Ask *What two ideas are the focus of the second paragraph?* (Testing and interviews about testing.)

- In paragraph two, tell students to examine the first set of highlighted words. Ask: Why is the passive used in the second sentence? (To keep the focus on testing.) Direct the students to read the call-out box and discuss as necessary.

- Finally, have students examine the second set of highlighted words. Ask students if they can explain why the author shifts to the passive again. (To keep the focus on interviews.)

- Ask groups to prepare a single-paragraph summary of the information they gathered as a group. This summary should include at least one active-to-passive shift and be composed in an academic tone.

- Have groups exchange summaries for peer-editing. Ask students to note any active-to-passive shifts and to comment on the tone of the summary. Call on groups to share their work and discuss as a class.

● ADDITIONAL ACTIVITIES

The purpose of this activity is to provide students with additional practice with the various passive verb forms in a reality-based writing activity.

- Tell students they will be writing a paragraph on a common health problem. Brainstorm a short list of common health problems as a class and allow for some limited discussion. Have students work in small groups to continue brainstorming one of the topics. Tell students they should draw upon their existing knowledge and brainstorm information that could be included in this paragraph.

- Circulate and monitor groups as they work. Provide students with suggestions for their topics, such as causes, demographics, treatments. Refer students to the Form, Meaning, and Use Notes in the chapter as needed (pages 76–78).

6 Nouns and Noun Modifiers

Overview

Nouns have many challenging features for students to master. They can be singular or plural, proper or common (e.g., *states, the United States*), concrete or abstract (e.g., *table, vision*), count or noncount (e.g., *pennies, money*). The use of nouns also dictates the use of accompanying articles, quantifiers, and other determiners (e.g., *He was playing in a tournament when he broke his arm.*) Nouns can be used as modifiers either singly (e.g., *leather coat, freight elevator*), in compound modifiers (e.g. a *five-mile race*), or in prepositional phrase modifiers (e.g., *a list of groceries*).

Form: Students must learn which nouns are count ,which are noncount, and which are interchangeable depending on the context. The key points for students are

* remembering not to use plural verbs or pronouns with noncount nouns.
* using correct pronouns to refer to nouns.
* learning the order of multiple modifiers before a noun.
* using singular nouns in compound modifiers (e.g., *a ten-dollar bill*).

A GRAMMAR IN DISCOURSE

Business Investment Worldwide: Costa Rica

A1: Before You Read

* Read aloud the directions for the exercise. Call on a student to read the title. Then ask students for factual information about Costa Rica: *Where is it? What languages are spoken there?*
* Have students complete the exercise individually. Remind students they should predict what is in the reading and not read the text for answers.
* Have students work in small groups to compare answers and discuss. Circulate and monitor as groups discuss.

* Call on students from the groups to summarize their discussion of the questions. Allow continued discussion as a class as needed.

A2: Read

* Tell students briefly to analyze the format of the interview and then to scan the first sentence of each dialogue. Call on students to give their impressions of the interview.
* Have students read the interview to find out about business opportunities in Costa Rica.
* Put students in small groups. Tell them to discuss possible business opportunities in Costa Rica and specifically to note those mentioned in the interview. Ask *What are your impressions of Costa Rica now? Are they different than they were before reading the interview? Why?* Briefly discuss as a class.

A3: After You Read

* Have students do the exercise individually and mark the places in the reading where they found their answers. Ask students to compare answers with a partner.
* Circulate and note any problematic areas. Discuss these as a class.

EXAMINING FORM

* Have students work in pairs to complete part A of the exercise. Students will write the highlighted nouns from the reading in the correct category. Circulate and monitor, assisting students as needed.
* Combine pairs into small groups and have them compare their work. Then have each group discuss the questions in part B.
* Call on groups to share their answers with the class. Discuss and allow correction as necessary.
* Ask students to identify any interesting characteristics of the highlighted nouns, such as affixes, suffixes, and *–ing* or *–(e)s* forms. Allow students to look back at the reading. Then draw attention to the word *tourism* and its suffix *–ism*. Ask students what part of speech this suffix indicates (a noun). Discuss as a class.

B) FORM, MEANING, AND USE 1

Nouns

EXAMINING MEANING AND USE

- Have students work in pairs to answer the questions (1. b; 2. b; 3. b). Give students a few minutes to refer to the Notes to check their answers.
- Call on students to read the questions and answer aloud. Discuss any disagreements and have students make any necessary corrections.

Overview: *Proper Nouns and Common Nouns*

- Have students read the Notes. Reinforce the information by asking students to match the example sentences to the bulleted explanations.
- Circulate and help students stay focused. Check that they understand the explanations by asking *Is this a proper or common noun? How do you know?*
- Call on students to brainstorm more examples of both common and proper nouns. Write these on the board and correct as needed. Discuss as a class.

Count Nouns

- Have students read the Notes. Then have students work in pairs to write new example sentences using singular and plural count nouns. Make sure they use at least one collective noun.
- Tell students to exchange sentences with another pair and then note any determiners used with plural or singular count nouns.
- Call on several students to write their sentences on the board. Prompt students to notice which nouns need determiners (singular count) and which to do (plural count and noncount). Discuss as needed.

Noncount Nouns

- Ask students to read the Notes. Then have students write new example sentences with both proper and common nouns. Circulate and monitor.
- Have students exchange sentences with a partner. Ask students to check the example sentences using the Notes and make any necessary corrections.
- Call on several students to write their sentences on the board. Ask *What noncount nouns end in –s? What determiners have been used?* Discuss as needed.

Nouns Used with Both Count and Noncount Meaning

- Have students close their books. Tell students you are going to read sentences to them. Tell them while they listen, they should think about the meaning of the noun in each sentence.
- Read aloud the first example sentence. Ask *Does this noun refer to something in general or to a specific example or type?* If necessary, elaborate on the meaning of the question and read the sentence aloud again. Discuss as a class. Repeat for several of the example sentences.
- Ask students to open their books and read the Notes. Answer any questions and discuss as a class.

Making Noncount Nouns Countable

- Tell students to close their books. On the board, write the nouns *advice, water,* and *silk*. Ask *Are these count or noncount nouns?* (Noncount)
- Ask *How can these nouns be made countable?* Prompt students by adding *a piece of* before *advice*.
- Tell students to think of as many ways as possible to make them countable. Discuss as a class.

C) FORM, MEANING, AND USE 2

Noun Modifiers

EXAMINING MEANING AND USE

- Have students work in pairs to answer the questions (1. b; 2. a; 3. a; 4. a). Give students a few minutes to refer to the Notes to check their answers.
- Call on students to read the questions and answer aloud. Discuss any disagreements.

Adjective and Noun Modifiers

- Have students read the Notes. Reinforce the information by asking students to match the example words to the bulleted explanations.
- Circulate and help students stay focused. Check that they understand the explanations by asking *What types of modifiers are often nouns? (Materials) When do you use* and *with modifiers?*

Trouble Spots

Some students may have difficulty remembering that nouns may serve as modifiers that precede other nouns. A good example of this confusion is *lot parking* (incorrect) in place of *parking lot* (correct). Make sure that students understand that these modifiers act as adjectives and, like other adjectives, they occur before the head noun.

Compound Modifiers

- Have students read the Notes. Have students write new example sentences using compound modifiers.

- Call on several students to write their sentences on the board. As students write, ask the rest of the class if the sentences are correct.

- Be sure to note any compound modifiers requiring an *-ed* or *-ing* ending and direct students' attention to these. Discuss as a class.

Compound Nouns

- Have students read the Notes. Reinforce the information by asking students to match the examples with the bulleted explanations.

- To help students understand the difference between the modifying noun and the head noun in compounds, practice with a few pairs of reversible compounds (e.g., *lamp table / table lamp*).

- Get students to notice that the head noun is on the right, the modifier on the left. Explain that a table lamp is a kind of lamp (*lamp* = head noun, *table* = modifier), e.g., *A lamp table is a kind of table.*

- Ask students *When can a compound noun be made plural?* Give examples from the Notes and discuss.

Prepositional Phrase Modifiers

- Tell students to read the Notes. Working in pairs, have students write six original sentences using noun phrases from the examples. Tell students to choose both singular and plural nouns, some followed by *of*, and some followed by other prepositions, and at least one example expressing possession. Encourage the students to use the noun phrases as subjects in some of their sentences, and to pay attention to agreement.

- Have each pair exchange sentences with another pair for peer-editing. Circulate and monitor to check that students are using the prepositional phrase modifiers correctly.

- Call on several students to write their sentences on the board. Discuss as a class.

D) WRITING

Editing: *Nouns and Noun Modifiers*

- Before beginning, review the term *subject-verb agreement*. Ask students to give examples of subject-verb agreement errors and discuss briefly as a class.

- Put students into five groups and assign each one of the items from the Editing box. Tell students to work as a group to plan a short presentation explaining the error in the sentence. Tell students they may include relevant information from the Notes.

- Call on each group to present to the class. First ask them to write the example sentence from their item on the board. After their presentation, allow students to ask questions and make suggestions. Discuss as a class.

Beyond the Sentence: *Avoiding Repetition Using Pronouns and Synonyms*

- Tell students to read the passage and identify the main point (that stamp collecting is an interesting and enjoyable hobby). Briefly discuss as a class.

- Direct students to scan the first paragraph and note the glossed words. Ask students how the first two glossed words in the first paragraph are related (the pronoun *they* refers to *Everyone* in the preceding sentence).

- Have students look at the next two glossed words and ask What does it in these two sentences refer to? Direct students to read the first call-out box and then discuss as a class.

- Ask students to scan the last paragraph and note the glossed words. In pairs, have students discuss how the glossed words may relate to one another.

- Circulate and monitor as pairs work and direct them to the remaining two call-out boxes before providing assistance. Discuss as a class and then read through the last call-out boxes.

ADDITIONAL ACTIVITIES

The purpose of this activity is to check students' understanding of nouns and noun modifiers by returning to the reading at the beginning of the chapter and applying what they have learned.

- Have students work in pairs to go through the reading on page 90–91 to find two or three different examples for each item in the list below.

- Put on the board a list of the different types of noun (e.g., *Proper Nouns, Common Nouns, Singular Count Nouns*).

- Circulate and monitor as students work. To reinforce the task or resolve any difficulties, prompt students by referring them to specific Notes. Discuss students' findings as a class.

7 Articles and Other Determiners

Overview

A/an and *the* are the most identifiable articles, but the correct usage relies on an accurate understanding of the Ø article. The indefinite article *a/an* can be thought of as equivalent to *one* when used in the first mention of a concrete, singular, or countable noun. The definite article *the* is used before nouns that are specific because of a previous occurrence (e.g., *A cat came into the house. The cat was very hungry*), that refer to common knowledge, that come before familiar or unique nouns (e.g., *the beach, the garden*). The Ø article is used before noncount nouns, plural count nouns, most proper nouns, and generic nouns. Some other determiners, such as demonstrative and possessive adjectives, can be used instead of articles.

Form: A major obstacle for many students working toward fluency is learning the correct usage of articles and determiners. Before beginning, consider having a short discussion with students to elicit their prior knowledge of the form and function of *an/an*, *the*, and Ø (some may know this as the "zero" article).

A GRAMMAR IN DISCOURSE

A Manifesto for a Livable City

A1: Before You Read

- Have students work in pairs to answer the questions. Circulate and monitor. Then combine pairs into groups of four and tell students to compare their answers and discuss.
- Discuss responses to the questions as a class. Then write *livable* on the board and discuss its meaning.

A2: Read

- Before reading, write *manifesto* on the board and call on students to explain its meaning.
- Ask students to scan the excerpt. Have them focus on the title, subtitle, first paragraph, and final paragraph. Tell them quickly to note any unknown vocabulary.
- After students have scanned the excerpt, ask them

what they think it is about.

- Have students read for detail, paying attention to unknown vocabulary. Remind them to infer the meaning of a word from the context and to use the glossary only as a way to check themselves.
- Review new vocabulary with students as necessary. Elicit how other students established meaning from context.

A3: After You Read

- Have students do the exercise individually and mark the places in the reading where they found their answers.
- Ask students to compare answers with a partner.
- Circulate and note any problematic items. Discuss these as a class.

EXAMINING FORM

- Have students examine the highlighted words in the reading. Ask students to note what these words have in common (they are all nouns or adjective + nouns). Call on students to give examples of words with *a/an*, *the*, no article (Ø), and other determiners. Ask students to give examples of words with other determiners (e.g., *these, our*) and discuss as a class.
- Ask students to work in pairs to do the exercise. Circulate and monitor. As students finish, combine pairs into groups of four. Have students compare answers.
- Write the following chart on the board:

A/An	The	Ø	Other Determiners

- Call on groups to write the highlighted nouns and adjective + nouns in the reading in the correct categories. Allow students to correct and also prompt students to identify whether the noun is singular count, plural count, or noncount.

- Discuss the exercise as a class and answer questions as necessary.

Trouble Spots
Tell students that no article (Ø) is used before the names of lakes, individual mountains, and names of leaders. The definite article, *the*, is used before rivers, oceans, and mountain ranges.

B) FORM, MEANING, AND USE 1

Indefinite and Definite Articles

EXAMINING MEANING AND USE

- Have students work in pairs to answer the questions (1. a; 2. b; 3. a; 4. a).

- Give students a few minutes to refer to the Notes to check their answers.

- Call on students to read the questions and answer aloud. Discuss any disagreements and have students make any necessary corrections.

Overview: Count Nouns and Noncount Nouns

- Have students read the Notes. Then have students write new example sentences for each bullet.

- Call on several students to write their sentences on the board. As students write, ask the rest of the class if the sentences are correct.

- Ask students to identify the bulleted explanation that each sentence supports. Discuss as necessary.

Indefinite Articles with Nonspecific Nouns

- Have students read the Notes. Reinforce the information by asking students to match the sentences to the bulleted Notes.

- Circulate and help students stay focused. Check that they understand the explanations by asking *With what kind of nouns can a/an always occur? Which articles are used to classify a noun?*

The Definite Article with Specific Nouns

- Ask students to read the Notes. Then place students in six groups. Assign each group one of the six categories (the labels in italics).

- Tell students that they will need to prepare a summary with new examples to explain their assigned information. Explain that they should use the bulleted explanations to help them prepare their summary. Circulate and monitor as each group works.

- Call on each group to present their information to the class. Prompt students to ask questions or make suggestions.

C) FORM, MEANING, AND USE 2

Other Determiners; Generic Nouns

EXAMINING MEANING AND USE

- Have students work in pairs to answer the questions (1. b; 2. b; 3. a).

- Give students a few minutes to refer to the Notes to check their answers.

- Call on students to read the questions and answer aloud. Discuss any disagreements and have students make any necessary corrections.

Other Determiners with Specific Nouns

- Have students close their books. Write *my book* on the board. Ask students to identify the possessive adjective and give more examples *(your, his, her, our, your, its)*. Write them on the board. Ask a volunteer to give another example of one of these used with a noun. Write this example on the board.

- Now write *this, that, these, those* on the board. Write the word *adjective* on the board, and ask students to give an example of *this, that, these,* or *those* used as an adjective. Write the example on the board.

- Tell students to open their books and read the Notes. Discuss as needed.

Articles with Generic Nouns

- Have students read the Notes. Then, in pairs, have students write new example sentences for the second and third bulleted explanations.

- Call on several students to write their sentences on the board. As students write, ask the rest of the class if the sentences are correct. Discuss as needed.

D) WRITING

Editing: *Articles and Determiners*

- Have students close their books. Tell them you will write incorrect sentences on the board and then call on students to correct them.

- Write the first example on the board but without the correction (* *It is important to research company before applying for job there.*). Call on a student to correct the sentence (add *a* before *company* and before *job*). Assist as necessary. Then ask the student to explain his or her correction and describe the error.

- Repeat as above with the rest of the examples. Then have students open their books and read the Editing box. Discuss as needed.

Beyond the Sentence: *Simplifying Previously Mentioned Information and Inferring Knowledge*

- Ask students to read the passage and identify the thesis statement: *The most obvious damage a hurricane does is the physical destruction, but it is often the psychological damage that does more harm.* Briefly discuss as a class.

- Have students read the first paragraph again and tell them to note the highlighted words. Ask students *How do these words relate to one another?* Then have students read the first call-out box. Ask *What does the highlighted word* they *refer to?*

- Tell students to read the second paragraph again. Ask students to identify the subject of the paragraph (Hurricane Katrina). Then ask students to identify what articles are used with the highlighted words *(the)*. Have students read the call-out box and discuss as a class, making sure they understand why the definite article is used.

ADDITIONAL ACTIVITIES

The purpose of this activity is to give students an opportunity to write about a topic of high interest to them. The activity also provides additional opportunities to reinforce the use of articles and other determiners.

- Refer students back to the reading at the beginning of the chapter.

- Explain to students that manifestos are usually written on subjects about which a writer feels passionately. Tell students that they will be writing their own short "manifesto" about an appropriate topic. Tell students to think of some controversial issues that they feel strongly about (e.g., whether trans fats should be banned in restaurants, whether voting should be mandatory, whether animal testing should be allowed).

- Have students analyze the format of the manifesto at the beginning of the chapter, noting its structure (e.g., use of "key ideas") and call on students to give their impressions. Discuss briefly as a class.

- Now ask students first to brainstorm and then outline their short manifesto. In their outline, students should use complete sentences and refer to the Form, Meaning, and Use Notes (pages 115–116 and 120–121) in the chapter to ensure they are using articles and other determiners correctly. Call on students to present their outline to the class.

- As a follow-up activity, have students compose their manifestos outside of class and bring to class for peer-editing. Make sure they refer to the writing checklist.

8 Quantifiers

Overview

Quantifiers are a category of determiners that indicate *how much* or *how many*. Quantifiers can function as pronouns or as modifiers. As pronouns, quantifiers can be modified by prepositional phrases. There are both negative (e.g., *hardly any*) and positive (e.g., *every*) quantifiers, those that modify count nouns (e.g., *few*), those that modify noncount nouns (e.g., *less, much*), and those used to make comparisons (e.g., *I have less money than you do*).

Form: Before beginning, review key terms such as *determiner*, *affirmative*, and *comparative*. The key challenges are remembering

- to distinguish between quantifiers that modify count nouns, those that modify noncount nouns, and those that modify all nouns.
- to identify negative quantifiers and to distinguish which quantifiers can occur in negative sentences.
- to use prepositional phrases before specific nouns.

A GRAMMAR IN DISCOURSE

Improving Lives One Click at a Time

A1: Before You Read

- Write the word *poll* on the board. Ask students *What is a poll? What are some common uses of polls?*
- Have students work in small groups to discuss the Before You Read questions. Ask students to make a short list of their main online activities. Circulate and monitor and keep students focused.
- Discuss as a class. Call on students to share their answers and allow each group to read from their list of online activities.

Cultural Notes

People in the United States are most familiar with political polls that dominate news in the months leading up to major political elections. Political polls are usually of high interest but may be less reliable than scientific or academic polls.

A2: Read

- Tell students to examine the title of the report. Ask *Has the Internet improved your life or has it had negative effects?* Tell students to make predictions about the report and discuss as a class.
- Have students read the report. Call on students to say whether their predictions were correct or incorrect.
- Divide students into six groups and assign each group a paragraph from the report. Ask each group to write a short summary of the information in the paragraph with an emphasis on any statistical information.
- Call on students from each group to share their summary with the class. Make sure students are including any relevant quantifiers from their paragraph. Allow students to ask questions and discuss as a class.

A3: After You Read

- Have students do this exercise individually. Tell students to mark the places in the reading where they found the information for question number 1. Then have them write a short answer to question number 2.
- Ask students to compare answers with a partner.
- Circulate and note any problematic areas. Discuss these as a class.

EXAMINING FORM

- Have students write highlighted quantifiers from the reading in the correct categories. Remind students that they will also need to write any accompanying nouns with each quantifier.
- Write the following chart on the board:

Followed by Count Nouns	Followed by Non-Count Nouns	Not Followed by a Noun

- Call on students to write the highlighted quantifiers with nouns in the correct categories on the board. Allow other students to correct any wrong answers.

- Have students work in pairs to answer the questions. Circulate and monitor. Then discuss as a class and answer questions as necessary.

B FORM, MEANING, AND USE 1

Quantifiers

EXAMINING MEANING AND USE

- Have students work in pairs to answer the questions (1. b; 2. 6; 3. b; 4. a).
- Give students a few minutes to refer to the Notes to check their answers.
- Call on students to read the questions and answer aloud. Discuss any disagreements and have students make any necessary corrections.

Quantifiers Before Noncount Nouns or Plural Count Nouns (1)

- Have students close their books. Tell students that you are going to read sentences to them. Tell them while they listen, they should think about the quantity of the noun in each sentence.
- Read aloud the example sentences with each of the quantifiers. Then ask: *How much or how many of the noun am I talking about? Is the noun in this sentence count or noncount, plural, or singular? What is the quantifier in this sentence?* If necessary, repeat or write the sentence on the board. Continue for each example sentence.
- Ask students to open their books and read the Notes. Discuss as needed.

Quantifiers Before Noncount Nouns or Plural Count Nouns (2)

- Have students read the Notes. In pairs, have students write new example sentences for each bulleted explanation. Circulate and monitor.
- Call on several students to write their sentences on the board. As students write, ask the rest of the class which bulleted explanation the sentence reinforces and if the sentence is correct. Discuss as needed.

Quantifiers with *Of*

- Have students read the Notes. Reinforce the information by asking students to match the example sentences to the bulleted explanations.
- Circulate and help students stay focused. Check that they understand the explanations by asking *Which quantifiers always occur with of? What*

sentence shows of *with a pronoun?*
- Call on students to elicit an example sentence for each bulleted explanation. Discuss as necessary.

Quantifiers Used as Pronouns

- Ask students to read the Notes. Then have students write new example sentences for each bulleted explanation. Circulate and monitor.
- Call on several students to write their sentences on the board. As students write, ask the rest of the class if the sentences are correct. Discuss as needed.

Vocabulary Notes: *Comparative Quantifiers*

- Have students read the information in the Vocabulary Notes. As students read write on the board:

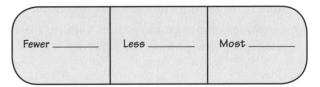

| Fewer _____ | Less _____ | Most _____ |

- Call on students to fill in the blanks for each of the comparative quantifiers: *fewer* + (plural count noun), *less* (+ noncount noun), *most* (+ plural count / noncount noun). You may begin by giving an example of each (*fewer books, less money*).
- Now have students give several original examples for each. Write these on the board and allow for self-correction. Discuss as needed.

C FORM, MEANING, AND USE 2

Each, Every, Either, Neither, and *Both*

EXAMINING MEANING AND USE

- Have students work in pairs to answer the questions (c, b, a, d).
- Give students a few minutes to refer to the Notes to check their answers.
- Call on students to read the questions and answer aloud. Discuss any disagreements and have students make any necessary corrections.

Each and *Every*

- Have students read the Notes. Reinforce the information by asking students to work in pairs to match the example sentences to the bulleted explanations.
- Circulate and help students stay focused. Check that they understand the explanations by asking

What kind of nouns follow each *and* every? *Can you use* not *with both* each *and* every? *Discuss answers.*

Either, Neither, *and* Both

- Ask students to read the Notes. Then place students in six groups. Assign each group one of the determiners *either, neither,* or *both.*

- Tell students that they will need to prepare a summary with new examples to teach their assigned determiner to another group. Explain that they should use the bulleted explanations to help them prepare their summary. Circulate and monitor as students work.

- Combine two groups to present their summary to one another. As groups work, circulate and prompt students to ask questions or make suggestions.

- Combine groups again to go over different material and repeat. Discuss as a class as needed.

D WRITING

Editing: *Quantifiers*

- Before beginning, review the concept of *most* and *most of the* and their general or specific meanings. Call on students to give examples with these words. Write a few of their examples on the board.

- Read through the Editing box as a class. After each example sentence, call on a student to explain why the sentence was corrected as it was. Discuss any questions as necessary.

Beyond the Sentence: *Referring to Quantified Noun Phrases*

- Ask students to read the passage and identify the main point (that e-mail has changed the way many people maintain relationships). Briefly discuss as a class.

- Direct students to read the first paragraph of the passage again, noting the highlighted words. Call on students to identify how these words relate to the underlined word.

- Tell students to read the call-out box on the right. Discuss as necessary. Make sure students understand the term *antecedent.*

- Ask students to read the remaining paragraph again, noting the highlighted and underlined words. Ask students *What does* some *refer to in the second paragraph? What does the highlighted word* others *refer to?*

- Have students read the call-out box on the left.

Discuss as necessary.

ADDITIONAL ACTIVITIES

The purpose of this activity is to give students an opportunity to conduct a short poll on a topic of interest to them, and apply what they have learned about quantifiers.

- Bring to class different types of polls, such as current event polls from newspapers, political polls, or pop culture polls from magazines. Distribute these in class and ask students to comment on them.

- Ask students to brainstorm a list of topics that are appropriate for polling. Ask *What types of polls have you seen before? Why do you think many people enjoy reading polls? What are the most common features of a poll?* Discuss as a class.

- Tell students that they will be conducting a poll on a topic that interests them. Have students work in small groups to brainstorm how a poll should be conducted. Circulate and monitor and make suggestions as needed.

- Have students work individually to brainstorm a topic along with several questions for their poll. Combine students into pairs and have them compare topics and questions. Have students make suggestions for revisions.

- Allow students to circulate in class and use their poll to survey other students. Alternatively, students may do their polling outside of class.

- Have students summarize the data from their poll in a paragraph. Tell students to include appropriate quantifiers in their summary. Refer students to the Notes in the chapter as needed (pages 134–136 and 140–141).

- Call on students to share their summaries with the class.

CHAPTER

9 Gerunds and Infinitives

Overview

Gerunds can look at first glance like continuous verbs. Both infinitives and gerunds can be challenging when used in their perfect forms, and when used in various positions in sentences (as subjects, objects, complements, etc.). Gerunds (but not infinitives) can also be the objects of prepositions. Both forms can follow several parts of speech, such as nouns, pronouns, adjectives, or verbs.

Form: The key challenges are remembering

- which verbs (and sometimes nouns and adjectives) are customarily followed by a gerund and which ones by an infinitive.
- which verbs can be followed by either a gerund or an infinitive but with a change in meaning.
- that both gerunds and infinitives can be preceded or followed by objects.

A GRAMMAR IN DISCOURSE

Overwork in America

A1: Before You Read

- Ask students to freewrite for five minutes on the topic of work. Ask *What is your attitude toward work?*
- Discuss the questions. Then call on students to share both their freewriting observations and their answers with the class.

Cultural Notes

Explain that some business professionals in the United States may work as many as 60 or more hours a week. This is known as "workaholism" and may sometimes result in physical and psychological problems.

A2: Read

- Ask students to scan the excerpt for any unfamiliar vocabulary (glossed or unglossed). Elicit this vocabulary from the students and write the words on the board.
- Encourage students to use the context or to analyze word parts to resolve unknown vocabulary while reading.
- Ask students to read the excerpt once for general meaning. Then put students in small groups and assign one of the three numbered points in the research study (*Lack of Focus, Low-Value Work*, and *Accessibility Outside the Office*) to each group. Tell them to read the relevant part and then brainstorm possible solutions to the problem. Discuss as a class.

A3: After You Read

- In pairs, have students read and discuss the questions.
- Circulate and monitor for difficulties.
- Allow time for the whole class to share and discuss. Be generous with time for the last question. Answers to this question will vary from student to student and will provide an opportunity for sharing ideas and experience as well as practicing oral skills.

Trouble Spots
Point out to students that gerunds and present participles, which share the same form in English, have different uses: gerunds as nouns and participles as modifiers.

EXAMINING FORM

- Ask students to locate the first example sentence in the article (paragraph 2: *tend to focus*). Make sure students understand where to put it in the chart. Then have students complete the exercise in pairs.
- Ask four volunteers to go to the board and write answers for each category.

B FORM, MEANING, AND USE 1

Gerunds and Infinitives

EXAMINING MEANING AND USE

- Have students work in pairs to answer the questions (1. b, a; 2. b, a). Give students a few minutes to refer to the Notes to check their answers.
- Call on students to read the questions and answers aloud. Discuss any disagreements and have students make any necessary corrections.

Gerunds

- Have students read the Notes. Reinforce the information by asking students to match the example sentences to the bulleted explanations.
- Circulate and help students stay focused. Check that that they understand the explanations by asking *How does the example sentence illustrate the explanation?* Discuss answers as a class.

Infinitives

- Have students read the Notes. Then in pairs have students write new example sentences for each bulleted explanation. Circulate and monitor.
- Call on several students to write their sentences on the board. As students write, ask the rest of the class if the sentences are correct. Discuss as needed.

Verbs Followed by Both Gerunds and Infinitives

- Write these verbs on the board: *continue, love, prefer, start, remember, forget.* Have students write two sentences for each verb, one with a gerund and one with an infinitive. Circulate and monitor as necessary.
- Ask students to read their pairs of sentences to the class. Have the class say if there is a change in meaning.

Performer of the Action with Gerunds and Infinitives

- Have students close their books. Tell students you are going to read sentences to them. Tell them while they listen, they should think about the subject of each sentence.
- Read aloud the first example sentence. Ask *Who is performing this action?* Read the sentence aloud again if necessary. Repeat for the rest of the example sentences.
- Ask students to open their books and read the bulleted explanations. Answer any questions and discuss as a class.

C FORM, MEANING, AND USE 2

Passive and Perfect Gerunds and Infinitives

EXAMINING MEANING AND USE

- Have students work in pairs to answer the questions. (1. b, a; 2. b, a; 3. b, a; 4. b, a).
- Give students a few minutes to refer to the Notes to check their answers.
- Call on students to read the questions and answers aloud. Discuss any disagreements and have students make any necessary corrections.

Passive Gerunds and Infinitives

- Ask students to read the Notes. Then have students write new example sentences with passive gerunds and infinitives. Circulate and monitor.
- Have students exchange sentences and ask students to first check the new example sentences and make any necessary corrections. Then instruct students to rewrite these with active gerunds and infinitives.
- As students finish the task, call on students to write a passive and its accompanying active version on the board. Correct the sentences as necessary and discuss as a class.

Perfect Gerunds and Infinitives

- Have students close their books. Write the first two examples from the Notes on the board. Ask students which two actions happened in each sentence. In pairs, have students order the two actions from each sentence, e.g., *Which came first? Which came second?*
- Circulate and assist students as necessary. When the pairs are finished, have them open their books and check their answers. Discuss as needed.

D WRITING

Editing: *Gerunds and Infinitives*

- Before beginning, review the term *parallel structure.* On the board, provide some examples of parallel structure errors (e.g., *My cats like to lie in the sun, sleep, and washing themselves.*). Discuss as a class.
- Read through the Editing box as a class. After each example sentence, call on a student to explain why the sentence was corrected as it was. Discuss any questions as necessary.

- Call on students to write their sentences on the board. Discuss as a class.

Beyond the Sentence: *Referring to Gerunds and Infinitives*

- Have students read the passage. Ask students *What is the main idea the writer is trying to convey?* (That collaboration is more effective than competition in motivating employees.) Briefly discuss as a class.

- Draw attention to the first call-out box. Ask students *What action or state does* the situation *refer to?* (Complaining about co-workers, ignoring e-mails and phone calls, even refusing to attend meetings.)

- Draw attention to the second call-out box. Ask students to find the word *it*, then ask *What does* it *refer to?* (Knowing their own personality type.) Ask students why the writer would want to replace the gerund phrase with a subject pronoun (Academic writing should be concise and not repetitive).

Vocabulary Notes: *Passive Verbs + Infinitive*

- Write the following sentences on the board, *He is expected to be at the university by ten. He is expected to give a lecture on Monday.* Ask students which sentence describes a state, and which an action.

- Now ask students to read the Vocabulary Notes. Check understanding.

- In pairs, have students write their own example sentences for two of the mental activity verbs, and two for the communication verbs listed in the box.

- Ask several students to share their sentences with the class.

ADDITIONAL ACTIVITIES

This activity is intended to give students an opportunity to use gerunds and infinitives in a formal business context. Supply a good example of a cover letter for a resume. Have a brief class discussion about what makes a cover letter effective.

- Tell students that they are going to write a cover letter to a prospective employer. The letter will need to gain the reader's attention to secure a job interview. Explain to students that a cover letter should highlight a candidate's strengths, skills, and abilities. It should also state his/her career objectives and ambitions.

- Brainstorm some useful verbs with the students and write these on the board (e.g. *I hope, I intend, I would consider, I am capable of, I expect, I enjoy, I am interested in*).

- As a class, write several sentences using the verbs. Check that students are using appropriately formal language before they write the letter.

- Have students exchange their completed letters for peer-editing and revise as necessary. Refer students to the Notes in the chapter as needed (pages 152–154 and 159–160).

10 RELATIVE CLAUSES AND ADJECTIVE PHRASES

Overview

Relative clauses are also known as adjective clauses because of their role in modifying nouns. Relative clauses are one of the three major types of dependent clauses (with noun and adverb clauses). Relative clauses usually occur immediately after the nouns or pronouns they modify; however, those nouns can occur in any part of the sentence. Relative clauses also have their own internal grammar, usually focused around the connector (also called the relative pronoun). Relative clauses can be restrictive or nonrestrictive. Relative clauses may also be reduced to participle or appositive phrases.

Form: Before you begin

- review the key terms for this chapter, such as *noun, adjective, preposition, phrase,* and *clause*.

- have students survey the chapter contents page and discuss what they know about relative clauses and adjective phrases.

A GRAMMAR IN DISCOURSE

All About Einstein

A1: Before You Read

- Write the word *genius* on the board. Ask students to write a list of words they associate with the word *genius*. Then call on students to share their lists and write some examples on the board.

- Have students work in small groups to discuss the Before You Read questions. Circulate and monitor to keep students focused.

- Discuss as a class. Ask *How do the words you associated with the word* genius *relate to your answers?*

A2: Read

- Ask students to scan the article. Have them focus on the title and the first sentences of each paragraph. Tell them to note quickly any unknown vocabulary.

- After students have scanned the article, ask them what they think it is about. Ask students what they already know about Albert Einstein and discuss as a class.

- Have students read for detail, paying attention to unknown vocabulary. Remind them to infer the meaning of a word from the context and to use the glossary only as a way to check themselves.

A3: After You Read

- Have students do the exercise individually and mark the places in the reading where they found their answers.

- Ask students to compare answers with a partner.

- Read aloud each question and allow students to respond. Discuss their answers. Prompt students to say where they found their answers in the reading.

EXAMINING FORM

- Examine the first highlighted relative clause with the students and complete tasks 1 and 2. Then ask students to explain why it is written under the relative pronoun + verb column in the chart. Have students work in pairs to do the rest of the exercise. Circulate and monitor. As students finish, combine pairs into groups of four. Have groups compare answers.

- Call on groups to share their answers with the class. Discuss and allow correction when necessary.

Trouble Spots

Distinguishing clauses from phrases or identifying different types of clauses can be difficult for students. To help those students less familiar with the structures, have them practice by labeling independent and dependent clauses.

Relative Clauses

EXAMINING MEANING AND USE

- Have students work in pairs to answer the questions (1. b, a; 2. a, b; 3. a, b).

- Give students a few minutes to refer to the Notes to check their answers.

- Call on students to read the questions and answer aloud. Discuss any disagreements and have students make any necessary corrections.

Subject and Object Relative Clauses

- Have students close their books. On the board, write the four highlighted clauses from the Notes (e.g. *who wrote the Harry Potter books*).

- For the first example ask *Who wrote the Harry Potter books?* Help students answer by completing the first example on the board. Now tell students to complete the remaining three clauses by writing full sentences.

- Call on several students to complete the clauses on the board. As students write, ask the rest of the class whether the sentences are correct or not.

- Now ask students to open their books and read the Notes. Then ask students to identify which relative clause on the board has a subject-relative pronoun, an objective-relative pronoun, and a relative pronoun that is the object of a preposition.

Relative Pronouns

- Ask students to read the Notes. Then have students write new example sentences for each bulleted explanation.

- Have students exchange sentences with a partner. Tell them to make any necessary corrections and then discuss with their partner. Circulate and monitor.

- Call on several students to share their sentences and discuss as a class.

Omitting the Relative Pronoun

- Have students read the Notes. Reinforce the information by asking students to match the example sentences to the bulleted explanations.

- Circulate and help students stay focused. Check that they understand the explanations by asking *In what type of clauses can the relative pronoun be omitted with no change in meaning? What do you do if there are two object relative clauses in a row?* Discuss as a class.

Restrictive vs. Nonrestrictive Relative Clauses

- Tell students to read the Notes. Then put students into four groups and assign each group either *Restrictive Relative Clauses* or *Nonrestrictive Relative Clauses*. Tell each group they will present a brief summary to another group. Ask them to write new example sentences and explain the bulleted explanations. Circulate and monitor.

- Combine pairs so that each is presenting one of the two clause types from the Notes. Discuss any problematic areas with the class.

Other Relative Pronouns

- Ask students to read the Notes. Then have students work in pairs to write new example sentences for each bulleted explanation.

- Call on several students to write their sentences on the board. As students write, ask the rest of the class if the sentences are correct. Discuss as needed.

Adjective Phrases

EXAMINING MEANING AND USE

- Have students work in pairs to answer the questions (1. The guy was rude; 2. You should speak to one person; 3. My necklace is from Brazil).

- Give students a few minutes to refer to the Notes.

- Call on students to read the questions and answer aloud. Discuss any disagreements and have students make any necessary corrections.

Adjective Phrases from Clauses with *Be*

- Have students close their books. Write the first example sentence on the board but include the crossed-out text (e.g., *Only people who are on the guest list will be allowed to enter*).

- Call on students to identify the subject of this sentence *(people)*. Then ask them what information identifies the subject *(on the guest list)*. Now cross out the words *who are*. Explain that these words can sometimes be omitted with subject relative clauses.

- Have students open their books and read the Notes. Discuss as needed.

Adjective Phrases from Clauses with Other Verbs

- Have students read the Notes. Reinforce the information by asking students to match the example sentences to the bulleted explanations.

- Circulate and help students stay focused. Check that they understand the explanations by asking *When is it not possible to reduce a relative clause with a verb other than be?* Discuss as a class.

D WRITING

Editing: *Relative Clauses*

- Have students close their books. Tell them you will write incorrect sentences on the board and then call on students to correct them.

- Write the first example on the board but without the correction (* *He's the writer whose books is on all the bestseller lists*). Call on a student to correct the sentence (replace *is* with *are*). Assist as necessary. Then ask the student to explain his or her correction and describe the error.

- Repeat as above with the next five examples. Then have students open their books and read the Editing box. Discuss as needed.

Beyond the Sentence: *Defining Nouns and Adding Information*

- Ask students to read the passage and identify the main point (that there are many ways to define a good leader). Briefly discuss as a class.

- Have students read the first paragraph again and tell them to note the underlined and highlighted words. Ask students *How does the underlined word* someone *relate to the following highlighted words? Why would a writer use a relative clause to define a noun?* Then direct students to read the first and second call-out boxes. Discuss as needed.

- Tell students to read the second paragraph again. Ask students to think about the underlined and highlighted words. Ask *What background information is given in this paragraph?* Call on students to give examples. Direct students to read the last call-out box and discuss as a class.

ADDITIONAL ACTIVITIES

The purpose of this activity is to give students practice using the different types of relative clauses and adjective phrases from the chapter.

- Tell students that they will brainstorm details for two to three fictional people. Copy the following chart onto the board:

Name	Hobbies	Favorites	Appearance

- As a class, brainstorm a description of one fictional person. Begin by eliciting a name from students and then adding information to each column of the chart (e.g., *hobbies: skiing, photography*).

- With that information, write one or two example sentences with relative clauses on the board.

- Now have students work in small groups to create their own chart with information for two to three fictional people. Circulate and monitor as groups work.

- Have students exchange charts with another group and generate as many sentences as possible using the different types of relative clauses and adjective phrases from this chapter. Refer students to the Notes in the chapter as needed (pages 172–175 and 181–182).

- Call on students from each group to share their sentences describing the people from the other group's chart. Discuss any problematic areas as necessary.

11 Coordinating Conjunctions and Transitions

Overview

Coordinating conjunctions (*and, or, but, yet, nor,* etc.) are connectors that indicate specific relationships between ideas within a sentence. They produce compound sentences in which the connected ideas have equal significance. Transitions connect ideas between related sentences and are usually placed in the second of the two connected sentences. Alternatively, they can occur within the second sentence but with different punctuation.

Form: Before you begin the chapter, you may want to

- review key terms from the chapter, such as *clause, phrase, independent, dependent, compound.*
- discuss the correct usage of punctuation, notably the period (.), comma (,), and semicolon (;).

A GRAMMAR IN DISCOURSE

Kiss and Make Up

A1: Before You Read

- Call on a student to read the first question aloud. Write the phrase *conflict resolution* on the board. Ask what the phrase means. Then discuss the first question as a class.
- Call on another student to read the second set of questions aloud. Have students work in small groups to discuss. Circulate and monitor to help students stay focused.
- Discuss as a class. Ask students how their explanations of the phrase *conflict resolution* relate to the ways they settle arguments.

A2: Read

- Ask students to scan the article for any unfamiliar vocabulary (glossed or unglossed). Elicit this vocabulary from students and write the words on the board.
- Tell students to use the context and to analyze word parts to resolve unknown vocabulary while reading.

- Ask students to read the article once for general meaning. Then put students in six groups and assign one of the paragraphs to each group. Tell groups to read the paragraph and summarize the information.
- Call on groups to share their summaries with the class. Ask *How and why are conflicts resolved in animal groups?* Discuss as necessary.

A3: After You Read

- In pairs, have students do the exercise and mark the places in the reading where they found their answers.
- Ask students to compare answers with another pair.
- Allow time for whole-class sharing and discussion. Allow students to answer each other's questions.

EXAMINING FORM

- Write the following sentence from the reading on the board *Ongoing violence worldwide is incredibly destructive, yet we humans find it very difficult to stop fighting.* Call on students to identify the two ideas in this sentence. Then underline the word *yet.*
- Ask students to work in pairs to do the exercise.
- As students work, write the following chart on the board:

Connect Ideas in a Single Sentence	Connect Ideas Between Sentences or Paragrpahs

- Call on groups to read aloud a sentence from the reading with a highlighted word or expression. Ask them to write the word or expression in the correct category on the board.
- Ask the class to correct any misplaced words or expressions. Have students give examples for these words. Discuss as needed.

FORM, MEANING, AND USE 1

Coordinating Conjunctions

EXAMINING MEANING AND USE

- Have students work in pairs to answer the questions (c, a, b, d).
- Give students a few minutes to refer to the Notes to check their answers.
- Call on students to read the questions and answer aloud. Discuss any disagreements and have students make any necessary corrections.

Coordinating Conjunctions in Compound Sentences

- Put students into five groups and assign each group one of the headings (e.g., *Showing Additional Ideas*) from the Notes. Tell students that they will present their assigned information as a summary to the class.
- Circulate and monitor. Help students by suggesting that they write new example sentences, note any specifics about punctuation, and present an explanation of the bulleted explanation.
- Call on each group to present their summary to the class. Have students first write any example sentences on the board and then have students explain the information to the class. Discuss as necessary and allow students to correct or to make suggestions.

Omitting Words in the Second Clause

- Have students read the Notes. Then have students write new example sentences for each of the bulleted explanations.
- Call on several students to write their sentences on the board. As students write, ask the rest of the class if the sentences are correct. Discuss as needed.

C **FORM, MEANING, AND USE 2**

Transitions

EXAMINING MEANING AND USE

- Have students work in pairs to answer the questions (c, e, a, d, b).
- Give students a few minutes to refer to the Notes to check their answers.
- Call on students to read the questions and answer aloud. Discuss any disagreements and have students make any necessary corrections.

Trouble Spots

As transitions are often used in academic and formal writing, it is especially important for students to use them correctly. Excessive use of transitions can add unnecessary complexity to writing.

Overview: *Transitions*

- Call on a student to read the first example sentence aloud. Ask *What is the transition in this sentence? What purpose does it have?* (The transition *in addition* adds information to the previous sentence.) Repeat for the remaining examples.
- Now tell students to read the Notes and discuss.

Showing Additional Ideas

- Have students close their books. Tell students you are going to read sentences to them. Tell them while they listen, they should think about the ideas in each sentence and how they are related.
- Read aloud the first example sentence. Ask *How are these two sentences related?* (The second sentence adds extra information.) If necessary, write the sentence on the board. Now read the sentence again and ask students to identify how the two sentences are connected (with the transition *in addition*). Repeat for the rest of the example sentences.
- Ask students to open their books and read the bulleted explanations. Discuss as a class.
- Write these transitions on the board: *in addition, moreover, for example, in fact.* Have students work in pairs to write new examples with the transitions.

Showing Similar Ideas

- Have students read the notes. Have students work in pairs to write new examples with *similarly, similar to, likewise,* and *like*.
- Circulate and monitor as students work. Ask each pair to write a couple of example sentences.
- Discuss each sentence and its transition. Refer students to the Notes for help and discuss as necessary.

Showing Contrast Between Ideas

- Ask students to read the Notes. Have students write new example sentences for each transition in the Notes.
- Have students exchange sentences with a partner to check for accuracy. Circulate and assist students as they correct.
- Have students return the sentences. Call on several students to write their sentences on the board. Discuss as needed.

Showing a Result

- Have students read the Notes. Reinforce the information by asking students to match the example sentences to the bulleted explanations.
- Circulate and help students stay focused. Check that they understand the explanations.

Showing Time Relationships

- Have students close their books. Write the first example from the Notes on the board.
- Ask students to identify the transition in the sentence. Then ask *How does the second sentence relate to the first?*
- Tell students to open their books and read the Notes. Then have students work in pairs to write new example sentences with the transitions *at the same time, afterwards,* and *meanwhile.*
- Call on several students to write their sentences on the board. As students write, ask the rest of the class if the sentences are correct. Discuss as needed. Discuss as needed.

Showing Sequence and Organizing Ideas

- Ask students to read the Notes. Divide the class into two groups. Students in group 1 each write a paragraph using *first, second, third,* and *finally.* Students in group 2 each write a paragraph using *first, next, after that,* and *finally.*
- Call on several students to write their paragraphs on the board. Ask the class if the sentences are correct and if the transitions have been used properly. Correct and discuss as needed.

D WRITING

Editing: *Conjunctions and Transitions*

- Read through the Editing box as a class. After each example sentence, call on a student to explain why the sentence was corrected as it was. Discuss any questions as necessary.
- Have students work in pairs to correlate each error to any relevant information in the Form, Meaning, and Use notes. Circulate and monitor as students work.
- Call on students to share any relevant information from the Form, Meaning, and Use notes for each example. Allow other students to ask questions. Discuss as needed.

Beyond the Sentence: *Showing Relationships Between Supporting Ideas*

- Have students read the passage and identify the main point (that most dogs and cats socialize in different ways).
- Ask students to scan the text and label any coordinating conjunctions or transitions in the passage.
- Call on students to identify each highlighted word in the passage as a coordinating conjunction or a transition. Ask *What relationship is being expressed here?*
- Direct students to read the two call-out boxes and discuss as a class. Ask what new ideas are introduced with transitions.

Vocabulary Notes: *Point of View*

- Have students read the information in the Vocabulary Notes. Direct students to the list of adverbs and ask how these words could be used like transitions.
- Ask *What does the word* viewpoint *mean?* Brainstorm a list of appropriate situations when you might express a viewpoint. Write these on the board.
- Tell students to use the situations on the board to make statements followed by sentences using the adverbs in the box as transitions. Circulate and monitor as students work.

ADDITIONAL ACTIVITIES

The purpose of this activity is to give students the opportunity to use a variety of transitions and coordinating conjunctions in the context of a practical writing assignment.

- Students will write a short explanation of how to perform a task, such as a craft, job, or basic cooking project. Tell students that they should use coordinating conjunctions and transitions. Refer students to the Notes in the chapter as needed (pages 197–199).
- Write the following list on the board:

  1. specific examples of materials needed

  2. a series of steps in a process

  3. any cautionary observations

  4. their general advice

- As students finish, call on them to read examples of coordinating conjunctions or transitions used in their writing.

12 Adverb Clauses and Adverb Phrases

Overview

Adverb clauses are a type of dependent clause and provide the same general information as the adverbs *when, where, why,* and *how.* Adverb clauses are linked to an independent clause by subordinators, such as *because, although,* and *when.* Most connectors between adverb clauses and independent clauses show logical relationships. Adverb clauses may come before or after the independent clause they modify. If the adverb clause comes first, it is followed by a comma.

Form: The major challenge of this chapter is to identify adverb clauses of time, concession, and reason that can be reduced to adverb phrases. Before you being, review key terms from this chapter include *clause, phrase,* and *fragment.*

A GRAMMAR IN DISCOURSE

Exam Superstitions

A1: Before You Read

- Write the word *superstition* on the board. Ask students to freewrite for five minutes on the topic. Ask *What is a superstition? What makes something a superstition?*

- Have students work in pairs to discuss the Before You Read questions. Then discuss responses to the questions as a class.

A2: Read

- Ask students to scan the text for any unfamiliar vocabulary (glossed or unglossed). Elicit this vocabulary from students and write the words on the board.

- Encourage students to use the context or to analyze word parts to resolve unknown vocabulary while reading.

- Ask students to read the article once more for general meaning. Then put students in small groups and have them list superstitions mentioned in the article. Discuss these as a class.

A3: After You Read

- In pairs, have students do the exercise and mark the places in the reading where they found their answers.

- Ask students to compare answers with another pair.

- Call on students to give examples of superstitions. Discuss these as a class.

EXAMINING FORM

- Review independent and dependent clauses. Write these examples on the board: *Although the climate is pleasant in California* and *The global economy has changed the world.* Have students examine the two examples and discuss. (The first is a dependent clause and the second is an independent clause.) Ask *How can we complete the clauses?* Discuss the significance of the word *although.* (It is a subordinator. It connects the clauses.)

- Now ask students to do the first exercise. Circulate and monitor as students circle the adverb clauses in the reading. Assist as needed.

- Call on students to read aloud sentences from the reading containing an adverb clause. Have students identify the adverb clause and any subordinators. Write these on the board if needed.

B FORM, MEANING, AND USE 1

Adverb Clauses

EXAMINING MEANING AND USE

- Have students work in pairs to answer the questions (1. a; 2. a; 3. b).

- Give students a few minutes to refer to the Notes to check their answers.

- Call on students to read the questions and answersaloud. Discuss any disagreements and have students make any necessary corrections.

Overview: *Adverb Clauses*

- Have students close their books. Write the first example from the Notes on the board. Ask students to identify the main clause, adverb clause, and subordinator in the sentence. Read the sentence aloud again if necessary. Repeat for the rest of the example sentences.
- Tell students to read the Notes. Discuss as needed.

Showing Time

- Ask students to read the Notes. Write these subordinators on the board: *when, while, as, once, as soon as, until, before, after, since, by the time.*
- Have students work in pairs to write adverb clauses using each subordinator.
- Tell students to exchange lists with another pair and add a main clause to each adverb clause to make a complete sentence. Circulate and monitor as needed. Discuss answers as a class.

Giving Reasons

- Have students read the Notes. Then have students write new example sentences for each bulleted explanation.
- Call on several students to write their sentences on the board. As students write, ask the rest of the class if the sentences are correct. Discuss as needed.

Showing Concession or Contrast

- Have students read the Notes. Reinforce the information by asking students to match the example sentences to the bulleted explanations.
- Circulate and help students stay focused. Check that they understand the explanations by asking *Which subordinator shows more informal contrast? Which subordinators are often used for expressing factual information?* Discuss answers as a class.

Showing Place

- Ask students to read the Notes. Write these subordinators on the board: *where, anywhere, everywhere, wherever.*
- Have students write new example sentences using each of these subordinators in an adverb clause. Circulate and monitor.

Showing Purpose

- Have students close their books. Write the first example from the Notes on the board. Ask students to identify the main clause, adverb clause, and subordinator in the sentence. Then ask *What information does this clause give us?*

- Tell students to open their books and read the Notes. Discuss as needed.

C FORM, MEANING, AND USE 2

Adverb Phrases

EXAMINING MEANING AND USE

- Have students work in pairs to answer the questions (1. b; 2. b; 3. b; 4. a).
- Give students a few minutes to refer to the Notes to check their answers.
- Call on students to read the questions and answer aloud. Discuss any disagreements and have students make any necessary corrections.

Overview: *Adverb Phrases*

- Have students read the Notes. Reinforce the information by asking students to match the example sentences to the bulleted explanations.
- Circulate and help students stay focused. Check that they understand the explanations by asking *Do adverb phrases usually come before and after the main clause?* Discuss answers as a class.

Showing Time

- Tell students to read the Notes. Put students into three groups. Assign either *Present, Past,* or *Future* to each group. Tell each group to write new example sentences showing their assigned time.
- Circulate and monitor as students work. Have each group write their example sentences on the board. Discuss as a class.

Omitting Subordinators in Adverb Phrases of Past Time

- Have students read the Notes. Then have students work in pairs to write new example sentences for each bullet. (Tell students to skip bullet 2.)
- Call on several students to write their sentences on the board. As students write, ask the rest of the class if the sentences are correct. Discuss as needed.

Giving Reasons

- Have students close their books. Write the first example from the Notes on the board without the crossed-out material.
- Ask a student to identify the adverb phrase. Then ask *What question does this sentence answer: how, when, where, or why? What subordinator could have been omitted?* Repeat for the next example.

- Tell students to open their books and read the Notes. Discuss as needed.

Showing Concession

- Have students read the Notes. Reinforce the information by asking students to match the example sentences to the bulleted explanations.

- Circulate and help students stay focused. Check that they understand the explanations by asking *How does the example sentence illustrate the explanation?* Discuss answers as a class.

D) WRITING

Editing: *Adverb Clauses and Phrases*

- Have students close their books. Tell them you will write incorrect sentences on the board and then call on students to correct them.

- Write the first example on the board but without the correction *(The plan to develop a section of downtown is moving forward. Because the city council approved the plan)*. Call on a student to correct the sentence. Assist as necessary. Then ask the student to explain his or her correction and describe the error.

- Repeat as above with the rest of the examples. Then have students open their books and read the Editing box. Discuss as needed.

Beyond the Sentence: *Showing Relationships Between Ideas*

- Have students read the passage. Tell students that adverb clauses are crucial to writing an effective argument because they express logical relationships.

- Direct students to examine the first highlighted sentence. Ask students to identify the subordinator in the sentence. Ask *What type of adverb clause is used here?* Then have students read the first call-out box.

- Tell students to read the second call-out box and the corresponding highlighted phrase. Ask *Why does the writer use an adverb phrase instead of an adverb clause?* (It's more concise.)

- Have students read the last paragraph, noting the highlighted words. Ask students to explain what type of information is included in this adverb phrase. Discuss as needed.

Vocabulary Notes: *Avoiding Wordy Expressions*

- Have students read the Vocabulary Notes. Write the following sentences on the board: *At the same time as I arrived home, a heavy wind started to blow* and *For the reason that jobs are scarce, many people have left their native countries.*

- Discuss the meaning of *wordy.* Then tell students to rewrite the two sentences on the board by making them more concise. Ask them to use the Vocabulary Notes chart. Circulate and monitor as students work.

- Call on students to share their sentences with the class. Discuss as necessary.

ADDITIONAL ACTIVITIES

The purpose of this activity is to give students the opportunity to use the full range of adverb clauses and phrases.

- Cut sheets of paper length-wise and distribute to the class so that each students has several strips of paper. As a class, brainstorm some observations about a city or another place common to the students. Write these on the board.

- Call on several students to make adverb clauses out of the observations on the board. Explain that they are not making sentences, but only adverb clauses. Refer students to the Form, Meaning, and Use Notes as needed (pages 214–216, 222–224).

- Have students work in small groups to compose sentences with adverb clauses and phrases using the observations on the board on their strips of paper. Tell students to refer to the Vocabulary Notes in the chapter (page 233) and to avoid wordy sentences.

- Circulate and monitor. Ask questions to stimulate ideas as needed.

- Have students cut their pieces of paper in half between the adverb and main clauses. Shuffle the pieces and pass these to another group. Tell each group to try and match the main clause to the adverb clause. Call on students to read their combined sentences to the class.

13 Conditionals

Overview

Conditional sentences express and *if* condition and a result. Typical conditional sentences contain an *if* clause (also called the dependent clause) and a main clause (also called the independent clause). The word *if* in the dependent clause can sometimes be replaced by other connectors, such as *unless*. The two major distinctions in conditionals are between real and unreal (or hypothetical) conditionals.

Form: The major challenges students face with unreal conditionals are deciding when to use them and how to form the verbs in each of the two clauses they contain. Key terms from this chapter include *clause*, *independent*, *dependent*, *real*, *unreal*, and *hypothetical*.

A GRAMMAR IN DISCOURSE

Ask an Astronomer

A1: Before You Read

- Write the word *astronomy* on the board and discuss the meaning as a class. As some students may confuse this word with *astrology*, an explicit comparison for the class may be useful.
- Have students work in pairs to discuss the Before Your Read questions. Circulate and monitor. Then combine pairs and tell students to compare their answers and discuss as a group.
- Call on students to share their answers with the class.

A2: Read

- Ask students to scan the article. Have them focus on the headings. Tell them to note quickly any unknown vocabulary.
- After students have scanned the reading, ask them what they think it is about.
- Have students read for detail, paying attention to what questions were asked of the astronomer. Remind students to infer the meaning of a word

from the context and to use the glossary only as a way to check themselves.

- Have students work in small groups to discuss any difficult vocabulary (highlighted or not) and to infer the meaning of the words, if possible. Circulate and monitor and discuss any trouble spots as a class.

A3: After You Read

- Have students do this exercise individually and mark the places in the reading where they found their answers.
- Ask students to compare answers with a partner.
- Call on students for questions that they would ask. Discuss these as a class.

EXAMINING FORM

- Briefly review the different types of clauses students know and note their observations on the board. Point out that this chapter focuses on sentences with an *if* in a dependent clause and an attached main clause.
- Have students work in pairs to examine the highlighted words in the reading. Have students write these in the correct categories in their books. As students work, write the following chart on the board:

Present In The If Clause / Present In The Main Clause	Past In The If Clause / Modal In The Main Clause	Past Perfect In The If Clause / Past Modal In The Main Clause
If + Present / Pres DC / IC	If + past / DC / Modal IC	

- Have students add the answers they found in the reading on the board. Correct as necessary.
- Ask students to identify the *if* clause and present, modal, or past modal in the main clause. Discuss as a class.

B FORM, MEANING, AND USE 1

Real Conditionals

EXAMINING MEANING AND USE

- Have students work in pairs to answer the questions (1. a; 2. b; 3. a; 4. b).
- Give students a few minutes to refer to the Notes to check their answers.
- Call on students to read the questions and answer aloud. Discuss any disagreements and have students make any necessary corrections.

Overview: *Real Conditionals*

- Have students read the Notes. Reinforce the information by asking students to match the example sentences to the bulleted explanations.
- Circulate and help students stay focused. Check that they understand the explanations by asking *Can you include* then *with any real conditional? When do you use a comma with an* if *clause?* Discuss answers as a class.

Present Real Conditionals: *Timeless*

- Write the word *timeless* on the board and elicit its meaning. Discuss briefly.
- Ask students to read the Notes. Have students work in pairs to write new example sentences for each bullet.
- Call on several students to write their sentences on the board. As students write, ask the rest of the class if the sentences are correct. Discuss as necessary.

Present Real Conditionals: *Possibilities*

- Have students close their books. Write the *if* clause from the first example sentence on the board (e.g., *If he doesn't like to cook,*) and ask students to complete the sentence with a main clause. Call on students to share their sentences.
- Repeat for the following three examples in the Notes. Then have students open their books and read the Notes. Discuss as needed.

Future Real Conditionals

- Ask students to read the Notes. Have students work in pairs to write two new example sentences: one prediction and one planned future activity.
- Call on several students to write their sentences on the board. After students have written their sentences on the board, ask them to identify any possible errors in each sentence. Refer students to the notes as needed and discuss as a class.

Advice, Requests, and Commands

- Have students close their books. Tell students you are going to read sentences to them. Tell them while they listen, they should decide if the sentence is advice, a command, or a request.
- Read aloud the first example sentence. Ask *Is this sentence advice, a command, or a request? How do you know?* If necessary, write the sentence on the board. Continue for all three of the example sentences in the Notes.
- Ask students to open their books and read the bulleted explanation. Answer any questions as a class.

Mixed Time Real Conditionals

- Ask students to read the Notes. Then in pairs have students write new example sentences with mixed time real conditionals. Circulate and monitor.
- Combine pairs to compare answers. Assist as necessary.
- Call on students to read their sentences aloud for the class. Allow students to correct and discuss as needed.

Alternatives to *If*

- Tell students to close their books. Write the first example sentence from the Notes on the board. Ask students to identify any words that are similar to *if*. Ask *How is this word similar to* if?
- Have students open their books and read the Notes. Ask *What subordinators can be used to introduce real conditionals?* When students answer, ask them to explain how the subordinator is used.
- If necessary, have students write their own example sentences with *as long as, only if, providing that, unless, even if,* and *whether or not.*

Past Real Conditionals

- Have students read the Notes. Reinforce the information by asking students to match the example sentences to the bulleted explanations.
- Circulate and help students stay focused. Check that they understand the explanations by asking *Which clauses use past forms in past real conditionals?* Discuss answers as a class.

Unreal Conditionals

EXAMINING MEANING AND USE

- Have students work in pairs to answer the questions (1. a; 2. b; 3. a).
- Give students a few minutes to refer to the Notes to check their answers.
- Call on students to read the questions and answer aloud. Discuss any disagreements and have students make any necessary corrections.

Present/Future Unreal Conditionals

- Have students read the Notes. Reinforce the information by asking students to match the example sentences to the bulleted explanations.
- Circulate and help students stay focused.
- Call on students to read aloud an example sentence from the Notes and the matching bulleted explanation. Discuss as necessary.

Past Unreal Conditionals

- Tell students to read the Notes. Call on a student to read the first sentence. Ask *How does the speaker feel?* If necessary, write *regrets* on the board and discuss the concept as a class.
- Have students write three new example sentences. Tell students to exchange sentences with a partner for correction. Circulate and monitor.

Mixed Time Unreal Conditionals

- Have students close their books. Tell students you are going to read some sentences to them. Tell them while they listen, they should think about the time for the *if* clause and the main clause.
- Read aloud the first example sentence from the Notes. Ask *What time is used in the* if *clause and in the main clause?* Then call on students to respond to the meaning of the sentence. Repeat for the second example sentence.
- Ask students to open their books and read the bulleted explanations. Answer any questions and discuss as a class.

As if and *As though*

- Tell students to read the Notes. As students read, write the first example sentence from the Notes on the board.

- Call on a student to identify the main clause in the sentence by underlining it. Correct as needed. Now call on another student to circle the dependent clause. Ask *Why is the past tense used after* as if/as though? Discuss as needed.

D WRITING

Editing: *Conditional Sentences*

- Read through the Editing box as a class. After each example sentence, call on a student to explain why the sentence was corrected as it was. Discuss any questions as necessary.
- Tell students you are going to write incorrect sentences on the board and then call on students to correct them. Copy the following sentences on to the board:
  - *I walk to school daily. As long as it's not raining.*
  - *If I would have done my homework, I would have gotten a better grade.*
  - *If I have had the money, I would buy a new car.*
  - *The weather is warm if I study in the courtyard.*
- Tell students to think about the examples in the Editing box. Then call on students to correct each sentence on the board. Ask *Which item in the box has a similar error?* Discuss as needed.

Beyond the Sentence: *Using Implied Conditionals*

- Tell students to read the passage and identify the main point (that if people made basic changes in behavior, the amount of garbage produced would be reduced). Briefly discuss as a class.
- Direct students to scan the second paragraph of the passage, noting the highlighted and underlined words.
- Then read aloud the sentence *Less packaging would mean less garbage.* Call on students to identify the *if* condition that this sentence refers to (*If corporations used less packaging*). Then direct students to read the first call-out box.
- Have students scan the last paragraph of the passage, noting the highlighted and underlined words. Ask *What conditions has the writer implied?* Call on students to give examples from the passage. Have students read the second call-out box. Discuss as needed.

This activity provides students with additional writing and speaking practice using the conditionals presented in this chapter.

- Discuss the various uses of conditional statements as a class. Ask *In what types of situations are conditional statements useful?* Call on students to give examples.

- Tell students that they will be using conditional statements to consider some common problems, possible solutions, and then possible outcomes to those solutions. As a class brainstorm some common day-to-day problems that the students encounter (e.g., finding a job, studying for classes, saving money). Write these on the board.

- Put students into small groups. Tell students to decide on one problem as a group and then consider present solutions and possible future consequences for each solution. Circulate and monitor as each group works. Refer students to the Form, Meaning, and Use Notes in the chapter as needed (pages 240–243 and 248–250).

- Call on groups to summarize their problem, give possible solutions, and describe possible future consequences. Allow other students to make suggestions and discuss as a class.

14 Noun Clauses

Overview

Noun clauses are dependent clauses that require an independent clause to form a complete sentence. They use connectors such as *that, who, what, where, when, how,* and *if*. Noun clauses act as nouns: as subjects of sentences, objects of verbs, objects of prepositions, and as subject complements after linking verbs. Noun clauses are common in indirect (embedded) questions (e.g., *Susan asked how my mother was.*).

Form: The major challenge for students is keeping statement word order in embedded questions. Key terms from this chapter include: *subject, object, complement, preposition, subjunctive.*

A GRAMMAR IN DISCOURSE

E-waste

A1: Before You Read

- Ask students to read through the questions. Tell students to circulate in the classroom and to ask at least five other students for their answers to the questions. They should record the answers.

- Monitor as students circulate and offer to answer the questions yourself.

- Now have students work in small groups to discuss and compare answers. Tell each group that they will need to summarize their information and present it to the class.

- Call on each group to present their ideas to the class. Discuss as necessary.

A2: Read

- Before reading, write *e-waste* on the board. Call on a student to explain the meaning of *waste*. Then ask *What does the e- prefix mean in this word?* Allow students to give other examples of *e-* prefixes (e.g., *e-mail, e-book, e-card*).

- Now call on a student to read aloud the subtitle of the reading. Ask students to preview the text

by reading the title, the first two sentences of each paragraph, and then the conclusion.

- Tell students to read the article. Circulate and attend to questions or difficulties as they read.

- Discuss the article as a class.

A3: After You Read

- Have students do this exercise individually and mark the places in the article where they found the answers. As students finish the exercise, combine students into pairs to compare answers.

- As a class discuss the questions. For the final question, combine pairs of students to make small groups. Ask each group to come up with additional solutions to the problem of e-waste. Circulate and monitor as students work.

- Allow time for whole-class discussion, as needed, to provide the opportunity for sharing ideas and for practicing oral skills.

EXAMINING FORM

- Have students work in pairs and examine the highlighted clauses in the article and write them in the correct categories in their books.

- Circulate and monitor as students work. As students work, write the following chart on the board:

That Clauses	Wh- and If/Whether Clauses
In a sentence beginning with *it*	As a subject
After a verb	After a verb
After *be*	After a preposition
After a noun	After an adjective

- Call on students to complete the chart on the board. Allow students to ask questions and to correct any errors.

- Ask students *What connectors are used in these sentences?* Note these on the board in a separate area. Discuss as necessary.

B) FORM, MEANING, AND USE

Noun Clauses

EXAMINING MEANING AND USE

- Have students work in pairs to answer the questions (1. b; 2. a; 3. b; 4. b).
- Give students a few minutes to refer to the Notes to check their answers.
- Call on students to read the questions and answer aloud. Discuss any disagreements and have students make any necessary corrections.

Overview: *Noun Clauses*

- Have students read the Notes. Reinforce the information by asking students to match the example sentences to the explanations in bullets.
- Circulate and help students stay focused. Check that they understand the explanations by asking *How does the example sentence illustrate the explanation?* Discuss as a class.

Time in Sentences with Noun Clauses

- Have students close their books. Tell students that you are going to read sentences to them and that they should think about the main verb in each sentence.
- Read aloud the first example sentence from the Notes. Then ask *Does the main verb refer to present or past time?* If necessary, write the sentence on the board.
- Repeat for the following examples in the Notes. Then ask students to open their books and to read the bullets in the notes.

That Clauses

- Ask students to read the Notes. Then put students into four groups and tell them to write new example sentences for the four headings in the notes.
- Circulate and monitor and write the four headings in columns on the board: *Objects of Verbs, Subjects, Subject Complements,* and *Adjective and Noun Complements.*
- Call on each group to write their new example sentences in each of the four columns. Have students. Have students explain their answers by identifying objects, verbs, complements, etc.

That Clauses After Expressions of Necessity and Advice

- Tell students to read the Notes. Then have students write their own example sentences for each bullet.
- Call on several students to write their sentences on the board. As students write, ask the rest of the class whether the sentences are correct or not. Discuss the formal tone of these sentences.

Wh- and *If/Whether* Clauses

- Have students read the Notes. Put students into five groups and assign each one of the headings in the examples. Tell students they will need to prepare a short summary of each by writing new example sentences and presenting any relative information from the bullets.
- Circulate and monitor. Assist students in summarizing the information as necessary.
- Call on each group to present their summary to the class. Prompt students to ask questions and assist as needed.

C) WRITING

Editing: *Noun Clauses*

- Have students close their books. Tell them that you will be writing incorrect sentences on the board and then calling on students to correct them.
- Write the first example on the board but without the correction (**He knew what he wanted to buy it.*) Call on a student to correct the sentence (delete *it*). Ask the student to explain his or her correction and describe the error (the pronoun *it* is not needed).
- Repeat as above with the following examples.
- Now have students open their books and read the Editing box. Discuss as necessary.

Beyond the Sentence: *Introducing Ideas Clearly and Concisely*

- Ask students to read the passage and identify the main point. (Before choosing a music instrument, it is important to consider several issues.) Briefly discuss the passage.
- Have students read the first paragraph and again ask them to note the highlighted words. Ask students *How do the highlighted clauses relate to the main idea?* Have students read the first callout box and discuss as necessary.

- Now tell students to read the second paragraph again and note the highlighted words. Direct students to read the second call-out box and ask *What does "What this means . . ." refer to in the second highlighted sentence?* Discuss as needed.

Vocabulary Notes: *Passive Verbs + Noun Clauses*

- Ask students to read the information in the Notes. Review with students the uses of the passive form. Call on a student to read the first example sentence aloud. Ask *What is the tone of this sentence?*

- Now ask students what type of information could be expressed with this form (commonly held beliefs). Ask for examples of topics. Brainstorm a short list on the board.

- Have students work in pairs to write a few example sentences for some of the topics on the board. Circulate and monitor as students work. Then call on students to read their sentences to the class. Allow for correction and discuss as needed.

ADDITIONAL ACTIVITIES

The purpose of this activity is to provide additional practice using noun clauses in a task-based assignment.

- Briefly review the concept of indirect questions with students. On the board write the sentence *I wonder whether he has a lot of money.* Call on a student to identify the noun clause in the sentence and ask *Is this sentence a question?* Discuss as a class. During the discussion ask students to think of situations where asking indirect questions would be better than asking direct questions. Write these on the board.

- Now have students work in pairs to practice using noun clauses with indirect questions for some of the situations on the board. Have students work for several minutes on writing indirect questions. Circulate and monitor. Refer students to the Form, Meaning, and Use Notes in the chapter as needed (pages 275–277).

- Call on students to share their indirect questions by situation. Have students write their sentences on the board and call on other students to identify the noun clause in each sentence.

- To extend this activity, tell students to brainstorm situations in other cultures where asking indirect questions would be better than asking direct questions. Then combine students into small groups to share and discuss.

15 REPORTED SPEECH

Overview

Quoted (direct) speech requires many changes for it to become reported (indirect) speech. Native speakers frequently ignore some of these changes, especially when speaking. When changing quoted speech to reported speech, the most common changes include: the addition of a connector (e.g., *that*, *if*, *wh-* words), changes in word order when the quoted speech is a question, changes in subject, object, demonstrative, and possessive pronouns, and changes in the form of verbs. These changes may require extensive practice.

Form: The major challenges involve changes in verb forms (since these changes often depend on intended meaning), pronoun changes, and using the correct word order. Key terms for this chapter include *imperatives*, *subjunctive*, and *paraphrase*.

A GRAMMAR IN DISCOURSE

Pinocchio's Nose or the Art of Lying

A1: *Before You Read*

- Read aloud the directions for the exercise. Have students work in small groups to discuss the questions.
- Call on students from the groups to summarize their discussion of the questions. Allow continued discussion as a class as necessary.

A2: *Read*

- Tell students to examine the title of the report. Ask *Is there an art to lying?* Briefly discuss and ask students to make predictions about the reading.
- Now ask students to scan the article. Have them focus on the title, the first two sentences of each paragraph, and the conclusion. Tell them quickly to note any unknown vocabulary.
- After students have scanned the article ask them to comment on the predictions they made earlier.
- Have students read for detail, paying attention to unknown vocabulary. Remind them to infer the

meaning of a word from the context and to use the glossary only as a way to check themselves.
- Discuss the article as a class.

A3: *After You Read*

- Have students do the exercise in pairs and mark the places in the reading where they found their answers.
- Ask students to compare answers with another pair.
- As a class, discuss the questions. Focus on the last question for an extended class discussion. Ask students *Who is Pinocchio?* Discuss any similar stories or fables regarding lying.

EXAMINING FORM

- Have students examine the highlighted words in the reading. Then ask students to briefly give examples of reported or quoted speech in the reading.
- On the board write *Michel de Montaigne said that lies came in all sorts of shapes and sizes.* Call on students to speculate about what Montaigne's actual (direct) speech might have been (e.g., "Lies come in all sorts of shapes and sizes."). Elicit other examples of reported (indirect) speech from the reading and discuss.
- Now direct students to work in pairs to do the exercise. Circulate and monitor. As students work, write the following chart on the board:

Present in the Reporting Clause	Past in the Reporting Clause

- Have students add the examples of reported speech they found in the reading on the board in the correct categories. Allow students to correct as necessary.
- Discuss the exercise as a class. Answer questions as necessary. Ask students what the tense of each noun clause is.

B) FORM, MEANING, AND USE

Reported Speech

EXAMINING MEANING AND USE

- Have students work in pairs to answer the questions (1. We asked Maria a question; 2. The computer hasn't been repaired yet; 3. Luis went home the day he said this; 4. I need to call Jim's boss.).

- Give students a few minutes to refer to the Notes to check their answers.

- Call on students to read the questions and answer aloud. Discuss any disagreements and have students make any necessary corrections.

Quoted Speech ⟶ Reported Speech

- Ask students to read the notes. Then have students work in pairs to write new examples of statements, *Yes/No* questions, and *wh-* questions first in quoted speech and then in reported speech.

- Circulate and monitor as students work. Have students refer to the explanations in bullets as needed.

- Call on several students to write their sentences on the board. Discuss as a class.

Past Tense Reporting

- Have students read the Notes. Ask students to practice transforming quoted speech to reported speech with a partner.

- Tell students that one person should read aloud a quoted speech example sentence from the Notes and then the other should transform it to reported speech. Circulate and monitor as students work.

- As a class discuss any difficulties students faced transforming quoted speech to reported speech and point out any common problems you noticed.

Other Changes in Reported Speech

- Have students read the Notes. Reinforce the information by asking students to match the example sentences to the explanations in bullets.

- Circulate and help students keep focused. Check that they understand the explanations by asking *When do you change subject pronouns in reported speech?* Have students give examples and discuss as needed.

Keeping the Same Verb Form

- Tell students to read the Notes. Then have students write new example sentences in reported speech for each of the five headings in the examples.

- Have students exchange sentences with a partner. Ask students to first check the new example sentences and make any necessary corrections. Then have students rewrite those sentences in quoted speech.

- As students finish the task, have each pair compare sentences. Call on students to write their new example sentences in both quoted and reported speech on the board. Discuss as a class.

Paraphrasing in Reporting Speech

- Have students read the notes. Discuss the meaning of *paraphrase.* Have students work in pairs to study the examples of reported speech in the notes.

- Tell students to note how the reported speech was changed from quoted speech (e.g., change in verb, verb tense, subject pronouns, omission of *unfortunately*). Discuss each example as a class and call on students to give examples of how each was paraphrased.

Present Tense Reporting

- Have students read the examples. Then have students write new example sentences for each bullet.

- Call on several students to write their sentences on the board. As students write, ask the rest of the class whether the sentences are correct or not. Discuss as needed.

C) WRITING

Editing: *Reported Speech*

- Put students into four groups and assign each one of the items from the Editing box. Tell students to work as a group to plan a short presentation explaining the error in the sentence. Tell students they may include relevant information from the Notes to share with the class. Circulate and monitor as groups work, providing assistance as needed.

- Call on each group to present to the class. First ask them to write the example sentence from their allocated error on the board. After their presentation, allow students to ask questions and make suggestions. Discuss any other related issues as a class.

Beyond the Sentence: *Combining Quoted and Reported Speech*

- Tell students to read the passage and identify the main point (that what is or isn't a lie depends on a person's perspective). Briefly discuss as a class.

- Direct students to scan the first and second paragraphs and note the highlighted words. Ask students to identify any quoted or reported speech in the paragraph. Tell students to read the first and second call-out boxes. Ask *What types of phrases are used instead of reporting verbs in these sentences? How are relative clauses and adverb phrases used in reported speech?*

- Now have students scan the last paragraph and note the highlighted words. Ask students to identify the reporting verb. Now have students read the last call-out box. Call on students to give examples of other reporting verbs from the box and discuss as a class.

ADDITIONAL ACTIVITIES

The purpose of this activity is to provide students with additional oral practice using reported speech in present and past forms.

- Divide the class into four groups, A, B, C and D. Tell each group that they will brainstorm a situation and then write a short script for a dialogue about that situation. Each group will be responsible for transforming another group's dialogue into reported speech.

- Circulate and monitor as each group brainstorms and begins writing. Help students with ideas for situations if necessary. Encourage students to use natural-sounding language and avoid extended, excessively complex language.

- Now call on Group A to perform their dialogue once without interruption. Ask Group B briefly to summarize the situation. Then ask Group A to repeat the dialogue and allow Group B to make notes as they listen. Then allow Groups C and D to perform their dialogue in the same way.

- Give each group time to transform the dialogue they listened to into reported speech. When they have finished, ask each group in turn to read out their reported speech versions. Make any necessary corrections and discuss any difficulties with reported speech as a class.

Student Book Tapescript

CHAPTER 1

A2 (p. 2)

Please refer to the article in the Student Book.

B1: Listening (p. 7)

A. Most American universities have foreign language requirements. Students usually continue languages such as French or Spanish that they began in high school. However, more and more university students are studying languages such as Serbo-Croatian, Korean, and Arabic. Government grants have made it possible for universities to offer a wide variety of less commonly taught languages. Because demand has been growing so much, many universities have added tutorial instruction and intensive summer courses abroad to their programs.

B. 1. I haven't seen Pablo around the neighborhood recently.
2. Don't you usually work part-time?
3. Where have you been lately?
4. How long is your class?
5. Are they still married?
6. You look relieved.

CHAPTER 2

A2 (p. 16)

Please refer to the article in the Student Book.

B1: Listening (p. 20)

A. An interesting new art exhibit has opened downtown. When I visited it on Saturday, no one was paying attention to the beautiful paintings. Instead, everyone was looking out the window at a crowd of demonstrators across the street. I still haven't learned why. Meanwhile, I had the whole gallery to myself for almost half an hour. It was really quite unusual.

B. 1. I saw John yesterday. He was reading a book about stress management.
2. As I was speaking to Ann, I became annoyed.
3. My grandfather was doing a puzzle and whistling a tune.
4. I had a car for ten years.
5. I was watching TV when we had a blackout.
6. I've taken an anthropology course.

C1: Listening (p. 25)

A. 1. He'd been waiting for me to call him back.
2. She's never traveled so far before.
3. What did they decide about the situation?
4. Ted hadn't run for a long time so he was out of shape.

5. We worked for hours and hours on the same problem.
6. By then, I'd had the car for many years.

B. 1. He'd been struggling for years until he found the job of his dreams.
2. I read the directions when I brought the appliance home.
3. I went to work even though I'd been feeling ill for a few days.
4. We celebrated all night because we'd managed to meet the deadline.
5. When he heard the news, he went on the Internet.
6. They'd already married by the time they graduated.

CHAPTER 3

A2 (p. 34)

Please refer to the article in the Student Book.

B1: Listening (p. 39)

A. Over the next three months, the waters of the Euphrates will be collecting behind the dam. In just over a month, the area will have become a reservoir, and two weeks after that, the newly discovered villa will have disappeared too. Is the story of Zeugma going to affect government policy? Only time will tell, but archaeologists hope it will make people more aware of the need to protect ancient ruins. Next month, officials from over forty nations are meeting in Turkey to discuss this important issue.

B. 1. I've never used this kind of equipment before.
2. On the first day of the dig, we start work at sunrise, and we work until about 11:30 a.m.
3. Tomorrow we're knocking down these walls to see if we can find the underground passages.
4. He'll have studied the report when he arrives at the site.
5. On July 1st, she'll have been living here for two years.
6. In the years to come, we'll probably be working with many of the same team members.

CHAPTER 4

A2 (p. 52)

Please refer to the article in the Student Book.

B1: Listening (p. 57)

A. In ancient times, astrology was often used by rulers to advise them what they could do. It was based on the idea that there had to be a correlation between events like famine or war and cosmic events. Unlike the way astrology is used today, common people were not supposed to use astrology. Instead, only their leaders could learn about their fate. Since a quarter of the earth's population still believes in astrology today, some interesting questions remain: How could astrology have lasted so long? Shouldn't interest have faded by now? What makes people think that there must be a connection between their lives and the sun, moon, stars, and planets?

B. 1. Am I supposed to attend the meeting?
2. We don't have to work on Friday afternoons during the summer.
3. You should have asked for a raise.
4. You might try dry cleaning that sweater instead of washing it.
5. Excuse me. Am I allowed to borrow these documents for my research?
6. My computer isn't working properly. What should I do?

C1: Listening (p. 64)

1. This horoscope can't be right!
2. The movie may not be playing anymore.
3. Maybe I'll leave work early tonight.
4. The robbers had to have entered through the back door.
5. The traffic shouldn't be heavy now.
6. Clara looks tired.

CHAPTER 5

A2 (p. 74)

Please refer to the article in the Student Book.

B1: Listening (p. 78)

A. 1. A: Is she going to college?
B: Yes, she's been offered a scholarship.
2. A: Did you get the job?
B: I don't know. I'll be contacted soon.
3. A: When are the pictures taken?
B: On Thursdays.
4. A: Did you have dinner at the party?
B: No. By the time I arrived, the food had all been eaten.
5. A: Why did you take the bus to work today?
B: My car's in the shop. It's being repaired.
6. A: Did you have your meeting with the boss this morning?
B: No, it was rescheduled for tomorrow.

B. 1. According to the radio, the storm began at midnight.
2. I was fined $50 in Traffic Court yesterday.
3. He's been awarded several prizes for his research.
4. Do you want to meet for lunch this afternoon?
5. Your suggestions have been seriously considered by the board.
6. The data were explained to the professor by her students.

CHAPTER 6

A2 (p. 90)

Please refer to the article in the Student Book.

B1: Listening (p. 95)

A. For the past few years, I've been visiting Costa Rica regularly for business and for pleasure. My trips began when I had a chance to start a business there. At that time, I quickly tried to find information about the Costa Rican economy. It was only by chance, however, that I also found a perfect place for rest, relaxation, and fun.

B. 1. What field will he be studying in graduate school?
2. What's the name of the report you were talking about?
3. How much clothing is in the drawer?
4. Did you put any honey in the tea?
5. Do we need any office supplies?
6. Do you still do gymnastics?

C1: Listening (p. 101)

A. Poor air quality is one of the major problems of well-insulated office buildings. Fortunately, a low-cost solution is widely available. Studies show that houseplants help clean indoor air. They remove toxic chemicals and they also add oxygen. Plants with fuzzy leaves may also remove smoke and grease particles.

B. 1. I looked at a first-floor apartment.
2. Where do you keep your boat?
3. I think they've found a cure.
4. Which of the guys was your roommate?
5. I bought a large round glass table.
6. Have you tried the test-generating program yet?

CHAPTER 7

A2 (p. 112)

Please refer to the article in the Student Book.

B1: Listening (p. 117)

A. A recent study of the new housing in the area shows that there are many barriers to building affordable housing. Not only is there a lack of government subsidies, but there is also limited land for new construction in the region. Developers need tax credits that lower their debt on construction projects. The subsidies allow them to offer lower rents to the public, and as a result, affordable housing becomes a reality.

B. 1. We had chicken and rice for dinner.
2. I'm looking for an apartment.
3. Before they moved in, they remodeled the bathroom.
4. I can't find my last savings account statement.
5. What is a marigold?
6. What's your favorite room in your apartment?

C1: Listening (p. 121)

1. What is the first chapter of your bird book about?
2. Did you hear that Anna quit?
3. What should we do first when we get home?
4. What did you injure in the accident?
5. What does Professor Jones focus his genetic research on?
6. Look at that painting. It's damaged.

CHAPTER 8

A2 (p. 132)

Please refer to the article in the Student Book.

B1: Listening (p. 137)

A. Many Internet users shop online, especially adults who have little time to shop. The majority of online shoppers are between the ages of 30 and 49. A lot of them appreciate the convenience and the large number of choices available online. Few seniors over age 65 shop online, although many would probably benefit from the convenience of purchasing some of their medications and groceries from home.

B.
1. We have plenty of milk.
2. How much work remains to be done?
3. I have little time left before I have to leave.
4. How many television programs did you watch last week?
5. Almost all the students passed the exam.
6. I can't find any salt.

C1: Listening (p. 141)

A. Purchasing a computer nowadays often involves choosing either a laptop or a desktop model. Neither of these models is perfect for everyone's needs, and each type has certain shortcomings. It's important for every consumer to find out both the advantages and the disadvantages of each from the standpoint of price, quality, and need.

B.
1. We bought four different pairs of shoes all at different prices.
2. Did you look through the large selection of coats?
3. She reserved either the noon or the 1 P.M. flight.
4. I read both books.
5. He was offered neither a raise nor a bonus.
6. My mother and father called last night from Hawaii.

 CHAPTER 9

A2 (p. 150)

Please refer to the article in the Student Book.

B1: Listening (p. 155)

A. Some employees can't imagine breaking all ties with work, even for a short vacation. They admit checking their voice-mail and even answering e-mails during vacation. Studies show, however, that employees need to relax and enjoy themselves on their vacations by fully removing themselves from work. Employees who can do this are much less likely to feel stressed when they return.

B.
1. I'd prefer John to become manager.
2. I don't like his working late.
3. We need to be working on the proposal when Tom calls.
4. Did you stop to buy the newspaper?
5. My goal is for you to learn XML.
6. We appreciate your helping us so much.

C1: Listening (p. 160)

1. Being asked to give presentations is common in Professor Anderson's class.
2. We expect to be contacted soon.
3. The client claimed to have sent us the check.
4. I hope to be offered the promotion.
5. I regret not being informed about the meeting.
6. Louise keeps being fired from her jobs.
7. We need the food to be delivered on Friday.
8. I deny having sent the e-mail.

 CHAPTER 10

A2 (p. 170)

Please refer to the article in the Student Book.

B1: Listening (p. 175)

A. In both ancient and modern times, the idea of dreams has been something that captures peoples' imaginations. A dream is a series of images, events, and feelings which occur in your mind while you are asleep. In ancient times, dreams were believed to be messages the gods sent to warn people about the future. In 1900, Sigmund Freud, who is considered the father of modern psychology, published a famous book which is called The Interpretation of Dreams. Today, people still believe they have dreams in which information about the future is revealed. Moreover, there are numerous reports of artists and inventors whose dreams inspire them, and many actually keep notebooks where they record their dreams.

B.
1. My brother who works in Seattle is a computer engineer.
2. Which shirt did he buy?
3. The woman I wrote to is named Ms. Lewis.
4. Where are you going?
5. Which restaurant should we go to tonight?
6. I think you have my notebook.

C1: Listening (p. 182)

A. Personal data assistants, called PDAs, are handheld electronic devices designed to help busy working people. These small devices, now considered essential by many in the business world, have become extremely versatile. The models made by all leading manufacturers help users perform many tasks including browsing the Internet, sending and receiving e-mail, playing computer games, and even making phone calls. A person using a PDA, therefore, may have a dozen electronic tools available at the same time.

B.
1. I heard that the woman from the accounting department moved.
2. Don't use a manual written in 1998.
3. Is there a reason why you didn't show up?
4. Tom's the guy from my neighborhood whose car was stolen.
5. Who's the person responsible for reimbursements?
6. Mr. Lee, a talented teacher and loyal friend, moved to China.

 CHAPTER 11

A2 (p. 190)

Please refer to the article in the Student Book.

B1: Listening (p. 194)

A. A day at the zoo may be a treat for you, but is it really paradise for the animals? This is a controversial issue, so let's look at the some of the most important pros and cons. Zoos provide food and shelter for animals, and they protect endangered species. These may sound like good ideas in theory, yet what actually happens at many zoos is another matter. Are the animals being protected or are they being kept from their natural environment? There is no simple answer, nor is there a simple solution. We're just asking you to think about it. For more information, contact your local animal rights advocacy group.

B.
1. I cleaned out the refrigerator and washed the floor.
2. It rained all day, yet they didn't cancel the event.
3. Hi Anna. I'm calling to tell you I'm stuck in traffic.
4. You can order pasta or you can try the fish.
5. The door was closed but it wasn't locked.
6. The contract won't be ready on Monday.

C1: Listening (p. 201)

A. Like any close-knit group in the animal kingdom, people who work together don't always get along. In fact, a majority of managers cite employee conflicts as a major problem. Training employees in conflict resolution, therefore, has become a big business itself. One Seattle conflict resolution center, for instance, reports that business has tripled over the last five years. "It's not that employees are fighting more," says director Mark Mason. "On the contrary, they're just more aware that something can and should be done about workplace conflicts."

B.
1. I have some good news. The city is planning a new animal shelter.
2. We've isolated the problem in the network and also added more security.
3. The tickets for the performance are really expensive.
4. Joe, like his mother, became a lawyer.
5. They have no batteries or candles and only a little food. Moreover, they're out of fuel.
6. Student athletes spend more than thirty hours a week on the field. Despite this, many excel in academics.

 CHAPTER 12

A2 (p. 212)

Please refer to the article article in the Student Book.

B1: Listening (p. 217)

A. Even though my brother denies it, he's really quite superstitious. For example, he always puts a lucky charm in his pocket before he leaves for an exam. Once a soccer tournament begins, he won't shave. He stays home on Friday the Thirteenth so that he can avoid bad luck. And of course, he won't walk under a ladder because he's sure that's asking for trouble. Whenever he's asked about this behavior, he says he's just being careful, not superstitious!

B.
1. My work became easier once I used a spreadsheet.
2. John called as I was falling asleep.
3. Everywhere he goes, the candidate attracts huge crowds.
4. I closed the windows so that the rain wouldn't get in.
5. My boss quit because she had a disagreement with the director.
6. The game is canceled even though the rain has stopped.

C1: Listening (p. 224)

A. Having just picked up our new car, my father parked outside our house. I stood there in awe, admiring every inch of it. Then without warning, a shower of salt landed on the car. I looked around just as my mother's

hand was returning to her pocket for more salt. "Stop," yelled my father, rushing to her side while explaining how the salt would damage the paint. Not interested, my mother insisted that bad luck could damage it more. Deciding not to challenge this superstition, my father permitted her to throw more salt. Though surprised at my father's reaction, I was glad that our new car would be "protected!"

B.
1. When did you see Sara?
2. Having studied for hours, Joe was really tired this afternoon.
3. I'm tired though still willing to go for a drive.
4. Before eating dinner, I sent the message.
5. While talking to Anna, I checked my e-mail.
6. Your plane doesn't leave until ten. Why are you leaving now?

 CHAPTER 13

A2 (p. 238)

Please refer to the article in the Student Book.

B1: Listening (p. 244)

A. If you drive a hybrid car, you get better gas mileage and you create less carbon dioxide and other pollution. Even if you can't afford a hybrid, however, there are still things that every car owner can do. First, if you get regular tune-ups, then you'll get better gas mileage and you'll pollute the air less. Second, you'll also get better mileage if you keep your tires properly inflated. Finally, drive at a medium speed whenever you can. If your engine works harder than necessary, it burns more gas and creates more emissions.

B.
1. Whenever I call John, his line is busy.
2. I can't leave unless the delivery comes.
3. Even if the weather clears up, I'm not going to the beach.
4. If I had a question about taxes, I used to ask Max.
5. If you're having trouble with your computer, you should reboot it.
6. What are you so upset about?

C1: Listening (p. 250)

A. Do you ever wonder what would have happened if you had acted differently at some important point in your life? Would your whole life have been different? What would your life be like now? If you had the chance, would you go back and make changes? Many people think they wouldn't make the same mistakes again. They act as though they know all the right answers now. Well, I'm not so sure.

B.
1. If I hadn't read the contract carefully, I wouldn't have found the mistake.
2. What would you have done if Tom hadn't been home?
3. I'd have an allergic reaction if I ate peanuts.
4. If I were you, I'd check the weather report.
5. It looks as though the plane is leaving on time.
6. I would've moved into a bigger apartment a long time ago if I had a dog.

CHAPTER 14

A2 (p. 262)

Please refer to the article in the Student Book.

B1: Listening (p. 268)

A. Whether we admit it or not, our reliance on electronic equipment is ruining the environment. The belief that new equipment is better and faster means that consumers are filling garbage dumps with an unprecedented amount of toxic waste from discarded electronics. As a consumer, it is essential that you be aware of this problem. Here are some suggestions about what you can do: 1. Find out where your local electronic recycling center is. 2. Decide whether or not you can repair or upgrade your old equipment. 3. Challenge the idea that newer is always better.

B. 1. You guys seemed pretty happy after the first tournament game.
2. I'm surprised that he left early.
3. I recommend that you be on time.
4. I've decided I'm going to get a new car.
5. The director has quit the project.
6. Let's talk about Anne. What do you recommend?

CHAPTER 15

A2 (p. 282)

Please refer to the article in the Student Book.

B1: Listening (p. 288)

A. A man said that he loved his birthday gifts. In fact, he was really disappointed with them. A child watching TV assured her father that she had completed her homework. She really hadn't. A woman told a caller that she had to get off the phone because the doorbell was ringing. It wasn't! Psychologists say that these are all lies. They claim that if a person intends to be misleading, then he or she is lying. Indeed, psychologists admit that these are small lies, often called "white lies," but since they are all attempts to deceive, they still fall under the category of lying.

B. 1. John assured me that he didn't mind helping.
2. He said he would come over the next day.
3. He asked if I needed any tools.
4. I reminded him to fill up the car.
5. He told me he had to find out the truth.
6. They reported recently that the discovery has important implications right now.

Student Book Answer Key

CHAPTER 1

A3: After You Read (p. 3)

1. Answers will vary. Some examples are:
Chinese is spoken by a large number of people worldwide, and it is also the third most commonly spoken language in U.S. homes. In addition, China is becoming a major world power, so Chinese will be important for business and politics in the future.
2. Answers will vary.

Examining Form (p. 3)

A.

SIMPLE PRESENT	PRESENT CONTINUOUS	PRESENT PERFECT	PRESENT PERFECT CONTINUOUS
begins ends shows learn rushes	is learning is growing are echoing are trying	has spent has skyrocketed have noticed has enrolled has designated	has been studying has been taking

1. Simple present: There are two forms of simple present verbs: base form and base form + -s/-es.
Present continuous: The form of the main verb is base form + -ing.
Present perfect: The main verb is the past participle form: base form + -d/-ed or irregular past participle.
Present perfect continuous: The form of the main verb is base form + -ing.
2. Simple present: There are no auxiliaries with simple present affirmative statements. (Negative statements use don't/doesn't and questions use do/does.)
Present continuous: The correct form of be (am, is, are) comes before the main verb.
Present perfect: The correct form of have (have, has) comes before the main verb.
Present perfect continuous: The correct form of have (have, has) + been comes before the main verb.
B. Answers will vary.

Examining Meaning and Use (p. 4)

1. a   3. b
2. b   4. a

B1: Listening (p. 7)

A. Most American universities~*have*~foreign language requirements. Students usually~*continue*~languages such as French or Spanish that they began in high school. However, more and more university students~*are studying*~languages such as Serbo-Croatian, Korean, and Arabic.

have made
Government grants~it possible for universities to offer a wide variety of less commonly taught languages.
has been growing   *have added*
Because demand~so much, many universities~tutorial instruction and intensive summer courses abroad to their programs.

B. 1. a   4. a
2. a   5. b
3. b   6. a

B2: Contrasting Verb Forms (p. 7)

Simple Present vs. Present Continuous
1. Do you speak   4. Do you have
2. are listening   5. hasn't
3. Are you having

Simple Present vs. Present Perfect
6. I've loved   8. We've lived
7. isn't   9. haven't looked at

Present Perfect vs. Present Perfect Continuous
10. I've been living   12. have you been reading
11. Have you visited   13. has won

B3: Comparing Simple and Continuous Meanings (p. 8)

A. 1. am thinking   4. has / is having
2. think   5. is looking
3. has   6. look
B. Answers will vary.

B4: Background Information and Present Situations (p. 8)

Answers will vary. Some examples are:
2. I've been working at the same job for ten years, so I know how to do my job well.
3. She hasn't eaten in hours, so she's pretty hungry.
4. I've lost my roommate, so I'm looking for a new one.
5. He hasn't felt well lately, so he's trying to take better care of himself.
6. I've already finished packing the boxes, so I don't need any help.
7. I've been working with a tutor, so my writing is really improving.

B5: Talking About Accomplishments and Progress (p. 9)

Answers will vary.

B6: Using Forms in Combination (p. 9)

Answers will vary.

B7: Thinking About Meaning and Use (p. 10)

1. ?   4. ?   7. ?   10. T
2. T   5. T   8. T
3. ?   6. F   9. ?

B8: Speaking (p. 10)

Answers will vary.

C1: Editing (p. 11)

1. Students of Chinese ~~tends~~ tend to have difficulty with pronunciation.

2. Many schools ∧are now teaching Chinese and Urdu.

3. Raoul and Carlos ~~has~~ have been working full time and ~~has~~ have been attending night classes.

4. ~~Always,~~ I have ∧always liked studying a new language.

5. Recently, I ∧have been playing guitar.

6. Chang ~~have~~ has not been traveling lately.

C2: Recognizing Present Contexts (p. 12)

Answers will vary. Some examples are:

A. ✓ The Internet has made shopping and doing business easier.

   X The classroom of the future is not necessarily a physical space.

  X / ✓ Learning a language has changed me in certain ways.

   ✓ My state (or country) is different because of the influence of other cultures.

   X I have traveled to many countries.

   X My teacher showed us several techniques for learning new vocabulary.

   ✓ There are many English words in my language.

B. Answers will vary.

C3: Talking About Your Life (p. 13)

Answers will vary.

C4: Writing Tip (p. 13)

Answers will vary.

CHAPTER 2

A3: After You Read (p. 17)

1. Answers will vary. Some examples are:

The writer was driving through Brazil when his car overheated because of a hole in the radiator. The people from a local village said they could fix it with green bananas. While he was waiting for them to fix it, he talked to a local man who told him that a nearby rock marked the center of the universe. Soon a boy returned with the green bananas. The hole was sealed with the green bananas and his trip continued.

2. Answers will vary. Some examples are:

His experience with the green bananas showed him that everyone and everything may have special potential. The rock helped him realize that everyone has a place that they consider the center of the world.

3. Answers will vary.

Examining Form (p. 17)

A.

SIMPLE PAST	PAST CONTINUOUS	PAST PERFECT	PAST PERFECT CONTINUOUS
forced gathered sent took	was straining was wondering was teasing	had (just) had had (never) paid had shown	had been wondering

1. Simple past: The main verb is the past form: base form + -d/-ed or irregular past form.
   Past continuous: The form of the main verb is base form + -ing.
   Past perfect: The main verb is the past participle form: base form + -d/-ed or irregular past participle.
   Past perfect continuous: The form of the main verb is base form + -ing.

2. Simple past: There are no auxiliaries with simple past affirmative statements. (Negative statements use *didn't* and questions use *did*.)
   Past continuous: The correct past form of *be* (*was, were*) comes before the main verb.
   Past perfect: *Had* comes before the main verb.
   Past perfect continuous: *Had been* comes before the main verb.

B. Answers will vary.

Examining Meaning and Use (p. 18)

1. b   3. b
2. b   4. a

B1: Listening (p. 20)

A. An interesting new art exhibit ∧has opened downtown. When I ∧visited it on Saturday, no one ∧was paying attention to the beautiful paintings. Instead, everyone ∧was looking out the window at a crowd of demonstrators across the street. I still ∧haven't learned why. Meanwhile, I ∧had the whole gallery to myself for almost half an hour. It ∧was really quite unusual.

B. 1. a   4. a
     2. a   5. a
     3. b   6. b

B2: Contrasting Verb Forms (p. 20)

Simple Past vs. Past Continuous

1. B: was having dinner
2. B: realized
3. B: were sleeping
4. B: fell
5. B: was holding

Simple Past vs. Present Perfect

6. B: I've known
7. B: I got
8. B: have never eaten
9. B: I had

B3: Simple Past vs. Present Perfect (p. 21)

2. No. The interviewee continues to work at the same job. It is not a completed past situation.

3. Yes. She joined the team at a specific time in the past, so the simple past can also be used.

4. Yes. The friend saw the movie at a specific time in the past, so the simple past can also be used.

5. No. The woman still lives there. It is not a completed situation in the past.

6. No. The friend is asking about an indefinite time in the past, not a specific time.

B4: Using Time Clauses (p. 22)

1. became, saw
2. was teaching, learned
3. applied, chose
4. left, met

B5: Describing a Past Event (p. 22)

Answers will vary.

Examining Meaning and Use (p. 23)

1. a She finished packing.
   b It's unclear that she finished packing.
2. b This focuses on how long it took.
   a This focuses on how much was accomplished.
3. b We began lunch and then she turned off her phone.
   a She turned off her phone and then we began lunch.

C1: Listening (p. 25)

A. 1. a   3. a   5. a
      2. b   4. b   6. b
B. 1. a   3. b   5. a
      2. b   4. b   6. a

C2: Contrasting Verb Forms (p. 25)

1. had been playing
2. attended
3. didn't have
4. hadn't arrived
5. had ended
6. checked, had been/was
7. had been waiting, arrived
8. hadn't studied/didn't study, was

C3: Giving Background Information (p. 26)

Answers will vary.

C4: Combining Verb Tenses (p. 27)

A. 1. The year was 1955. Rosa had been working all day [1] as a seamstress when she took a seat on a city bus. [2] She was tired.

2. She was arrested [2] when she refused to give up her [1] seat on the bus to a white person.

3. Rosa was a member of the NAACP. Before she was arrested [2], she had been active in the fight for [1] equal rights.

4. Rosa and her lawyers filed a lawsuit. Her case went all the way to the Supreme Court. She was still working [1] as a seamstress when the court ruled in her favor. [2]

5. She soon lost her job. By the time she finally found [1] another job as an administrative assistant, she had [2] been unemployed for eight years. [1]

6. After her husband Raymond died, she founded the [1]

Rosa and Raymond Parks Center for Self-Development [2] to help inner-city teenagers.

B. Answers will vary.

C5: Thinking About Meaning and Use (p. 28)

1. ?   4. F   7. T
2. F   5. F
3. T   6. ?

C6: Speaking (p. 28)

Answers will vary.

D1: Editing (p. 29)

1. When they returned to the city, it was raining and the wind ~~blew~~. *was blowing*

2. Al had *not* been ~~not~~ sleeping enough, so he *did* ~~not~~ do well on the exam.

3. How long *were* Professor Levine and his colleague ~~was~~ traveling in Brazil?

4. He was traveling and *leading* ~~lead~~ tours, ~~Until~~ *until* he injured his back two years ago.

5. The employees *immediatley* brought ~~immediately~~ a list of complaints to their new boss.

6. The team didn't finish their investigation or ~~announced~~ *announce* their findings.

7. By the time the storm arrived, residents of the coastal town *had* been evacuated.

8. Why *didn't* they ~~didn't~~ finish after they had eaten and ~~had~~ rested?

D2: Recognizing Shifts in Time (p. 31)

2. past to present   4. present
3. past   5. past to present

D3: Practicing Shifts in Time (p. 31)

Answers will vary. Some examples are:
2. Nowadays, I'm hardly ever at home on the weekends. I go the gym and then I go out with friends.
3. Now I limit my travel so that I can spend more time with my family. Now I can see my son grow up.
4. Now I always lock my door.
5. A few years ago, I only listened to pop music. Then a friend introduced me to jazz. Now I go to jazz concerts most weekends.
6. Now that I'm older, I look back on the many exciting times I spent with my friends and laugh.

D4: Writing Tip (p. 32)

Answers will vary.

CHAPTER 3

A3: After You Read (p. 35)

1. Answers will vary. Some examples are:
   The dam will produce electricity and provide water for a huge area of farmland, but it will also flood villages, remove 30,000 people from their homes, and destroy many valuable archaeological sites.
2. Answers will vary. Some examples are:

The mosaics come from a wealthy house in the ruins of Zeugma. They will all be sent to a local museum as well where they will be displayed.

3. Answers will vary.

Examining Form (p. 36)

A.

SIMPLE FUTURE	will become
BE GOING TO FUTURE	is going to produce are going to hear are going to clean 're going to remove
FUTURE CONTINUOUS	will be gathering
PRESENT CONTINUOUS AS FUTURE	is ending
SIMPLE PRESENT AS FUTURE	begins
FUTURE PERFECT	will have vanished
FUTURE PERFECT CONTINUOUS	will have been working

1. Simple future: The verb is in the base form.
   Be going to future: The verb is in the base form.
   Future continuous: The form of the main verb is base form + *-ing*.
   Present continuous as future: The form of the main verb is base form + *-ing*.
   Simple present as future: There are two forms of simple present verbs: base form and base form + *-s/-es*.
   Future perfect: The main verb is the past participle form: base form + *-d/-ed* or irregular past participle.
   Future perfect continuous: The form of the main verb is base form + *-ing*.
2. Simple future: *Will* comes before the main verb.
   Be going to future: The correct form of *be* (*am, is, are*) + *going to* comes before the main verb.
   Future continuous: *Will be* comes before the main verb.
   Present continuous as future: The correct form of *be* (*am, is, are*) comes before the main verb.
   Simple present as future: There are no auxiliaries with simple present affirmative statements.
   Future perfect: *Will have* comes before the main verb.
   Future perfect continuous: *Will have been* comes before the main verb.
3. Simple future, future continuous, future perfect, and future perfect continuous begin with *will*.

B. Answers will vary.

Examining Meaning and Use (p. 36)

1. a   2. a   3. b

B1: Listening (p. 39)

A. Over the next three months, the waters of the
Euphrates ∧will be collecting behind the dam. In just over a month,
the area ∧will have become a reservoir, and two weeks after that, the
newly discovered villa ∧will have disappeared, too. Is the story of Zeugma
∧going to affect government policy? Only time ∧will tell, but archaeologists

hope it ∧will make people more aware of the need to protect
ancient ruins. Next month, officials from over 40
nations ∧are meeting in Turkey to discuss this important issue.

B.
1. b   4. b
2. a   5. a
3. a   6. b

B2: Contrasting Verb Forms (p. 40)

A.
1. I'll sign
2. The cat is going to knock
3. She'll do
4. we get
5. I'm not leaving
6. I'll be relaxing
7. is going to start
8. will life change
9. will have landed
12. you'll have been working, I'll be happy

B. Answers will vary.

B3: Contrasting Simple and Continuous Future Forms (p. 41)

1. a, b, c   5. c
2. c   6. b, c
3. a, c   7. a, b, c
4. a, b, c   8. c

B4: Talking About a Sequences of Events in the Future (p. 42)

A. Answers will vary. Some examples are:
2. Once she buys a Spanish phrase book, she's going to study key vocabulary.
   She's going to study key vocabulary once she buys a Spanish phrase book.
3. After she checks the weather in Chile, she's going to make sure to pack the right clothing.
   She's going to make sure to pack the right clothing after she checks the weather in Chile.
4. As soon as she arrives in Chile, she's going to register at her new school.
   She's going to register at her new school as soon as she arrives in Chile.
5. By the time she finishes the program, she's going to/she'll be fluent in Spanish.
   She's going to/She'll be fluent in Spanish by the time she finishes the program.

B. Answers will vary.

B5: Making Plans with *Be Going To* and *Will* (p. 43)

Answers will vary.

B6: Making Predictions with *Be Going To*, *Will*, and the Future Continuous (p. 44)

Answers will vary.

B7: Talking About Future Goals with the Future Perfect (p. 44)

Answers will vary.

B8: Speaking (p. 45)

Answers will vary.

B9: Thinking About Meaning and Use (p. 45)

1. F
2. T
3. F
4. ?
5. T
6. T
7. ?
8. ?

C1: Editing (p. 47)

Hundreds of architectural and cultural sites worldwide are in danger. Across the world, archeological sites, valuable buildings, and works of art will disappear forever ~~Unless~~ *unless* we act now to save them. Many organizations are working hard to raise public awareness. For example, next month the World Monuments Watch ~~will~~ *is* going to publish a list of 100 threatened sites. In many cases if immediate measures are not taken, these artifacts won't survive. But if even only one site is saved, the organizations feel their efforts will *not* have been ~~not~~ wasted.

Money will be necessary. Unless the organizations ~~will~~ *are* be able to raise funds, they will not be able to rescue or ~~won't~~ protect many recognized historical treasures. Cooperation among nations, government officials, and researchers ~~are~~ *is* going to be even more vital. If society can rescue this valuable cultural heritage, then it will ~~has~~ *have* preserved an important legacy.

C2: Recognizing Shifts in Time (p. 48)

A.
1. shift
2. future
3. shift
4. shift
5. future
6. shift

B. Answers will vary.

C3: Talking About Plans (p. 49)

A.
2. vague
3. specific
4. vague
5. vague
6. specific

B. Answers will vary.

C4: Writing Tip (p. 49)

Answers will vary.

CHAPTER 4

A3: After You Read (p. 53)

1. Answers will vary. Some examples are:
People often want their horoscopes to be true and because the language used in horoscopes is very general, it is easy to find evidence to support this.
2. Answers will vary. Some examples are:
His horoscope warned him to wait until the full moon passed before he made any big purchases. By the time that had happened, someone else had bought the house. Dr. Bilton tells the story to show why people shouldn't rely on astrology.
3. Answers will vary.

Examining Form (p. 53)

A.

SIMPLE MODAL	CONTINUOUS MODAL	PAST MODAL
must get could be should (I) do might be can lead 'd better wait	may be coming	may have wasted shouldn't have relied could have had

1. Simple modal, continuous modal, and past modal: These modals do not change form.
2. Simple modal: The main verb does not have an ending. Continuous modal: The main verb is in the –*ing* form. Past modal: The main verb is in the past participle form.
3. Simple modal: There is no other auxiliary. Continuous modal: *Be* comes before the main verb. Past modal: *Have* comes before the main verb.

B. Answers will vary.

Examining Meaning and Use (p. 54)

1. a
2. b
3. a
4. b

B1: Listening (p. 57)

A. In ancient times, astrology was often used by rulers to advise them what they *could* do. It was based on the idea that there *had to be* a correlation between events like famine or war and cosmic events. Unlike the way astrology is used today, common people *were not supposed to use* astrology. Instead, only their leaders *could learn* about their fate. Since a quarter of the Earth's population still believes in astrology today, some interesting questions remain: How *could* astrology *have lasted* so long? *Shouldn't* interest *have faded* by now? What makes people think that there *must be* a connection between their lives and the sun, moon, stars, and planets?

B.
1. b
2. a
3. b
4. a
5. a
6. b

B2: Contrasting Modal Forms (p. 57)

1. ought to
2. had better have
3. should have stayed
4. were supposed to go
5. had to
6. shouldn't
7. have got to
8. must
9. can't
10. couldn't
11. may not
12. had to
13. don't have to
14. I'm not supposed to

B3: Choosing Modals or Phrasal Modals (p. 58)

2. had better / should / ought to / have (got) to
3. have (got) to / must
4. don't have to
5. are not supposed to / shouldn't
6. didn't have to
7. should have / ought to have

8. had to
9. weren't supposed to
10. couldn't

B4: Discussing Rules and Requirements (p. 59)

A.
1. must
2. cannot
3. have to
4. must
5. may not
6. must not
7. should not
8. may not
9. do not have to
10. do not have to

B. Answers will vary.

B5: Giving Past, Present, and Future Advice (p. 60)

Answers will vary.

B6: Making Statements with Modals (p. 61)

Answers will vary.

Examining Meaning and Use (p. 62)

b   I don't know if it arrived.
a   I'm absolutely certain that it arrived.
c   I'm certain it arrived based on the evidence.

C1: Listening (p. 64)

1. b
2. b
3. a
4. b
5. a
6. a

C2: Restating Sentences with Modals of Possibility (p. 64)

Answers will vary. Some examples are:

Present / Future Modals of Possibility
2. He should be playing on Friday.
3. He must not remember me.
4. Our trip can't be canceled / can't have been canceled.
5. Bill might / may be trying to call us.

Past Modals of Possibility
6. He must have known I was waiting for him.
7. He could / may / might have been lying. Or he might have been exaggerating.
8. By now, he should have found the note I left.
9. It can't have / couldn't have been easy for him to admit his mistake.
10. She might / may not have done it.

C3: Expressing Possibility About the Present (p. 65)

A. Answers will vary. Some examples are:
2. He can't be at the store. It's closed.
   He should be home. The clock could be wrong.
   He has to be on his way home. He may be stuck in traffic.
   He could be running some errands before he comes home.
3. Sean can't be home if he doesn't answer the door.
   Sean could be ignoring Ron.
   Sean may not be home. There could be a burglar inside.
   Sean must be in a bad mood.
4. It must be his birthday. Those are presents must be from his family.
   They could be something he ordered online—maybe a new computer.
   He might be starting a new business, and the boxes are some material he needs.
5. It should start up today if it started up yesterday.
   She may not be starting it up correctly. It might start

up differently than her old computer.
   The battery could be dead. Or it might not be plugged in.

B. Answers will vary.

C4: Expressing Possibility and Certainty About the Future (p. 65)

Answers will vary.

C5: Expressing Possibility About the Past (p. 66)

Answers will vary.

C6: Thinking About Meaning and Use (p. 67)

1. a
2. a
3. b
4. a
5. b
6. a
7. b
8. b

C7: Speaking (p. 67)

Answers will vary.

D1: Editing (p. 68)

   Deciding when to tell children the truth about Santa Claus can ~~to~~ be difficult for parents. Currently, as many as 700 million children worldwide believe in Santa. Many of these children have looked forward to Santa's visit since they could walk and ~~talked~~ talk. In addition, many parents think that children ought to believe in Santa as long as possible. They ~~maybe~~ may be having fond memories of their own childhood beliefs. They think, "Why ~~not should~~ shouldn't my children believe?"

   Older children in particular, however, may experience negative effects. First of all, parents ~~is~~ are supposed to tell the truth. If a child feels tricked, he may not believe anything they tell him for some time. Second, the child might ~~have~~ resent ~~resented~~ his parents, especially if his belief in Santa causes embarrassment.

   This is exactly what happened to Kevin Glover. Now 21, he still recalls the day he told his 11-year-old friends that he'd asked Santa for a bike. "They laughed at me," says Kevin. "I ran home and screamed at my parents for lying to me. I really think they should not have waited so long to tell me the truth."

D2: Reacting to Situations (p. 70)

A.
Situation 1	Situation 2
1. C	1. A
2. G	2. C
3. A	3. G

B. Answers will vary. Some examples are:
1. People are buying smaller, more fuel-efficient cars.
   Guess: People might be trying to save money on gas.

Advice: Automotive companies should pay attention to the trend.
Conclusion: This must be good news for companies that make large cars.

2. After World War II ended, there was a dramatic increase in the birthrate.
Guess: The government may have had to build new schools.
Advice: People shouldn't have had so many children.
Conclusion: People must have been happy that the war had ended.

3. The World Cup is gaining popularity in the United States.
Guess: Soccer may be more popular than football.
Advice: Soccer teams in other countries had better get ready for tougher competition from the U.S.
Conclusion: Immigrants to the U.S. must be influencing popular culture.

4. Last year 10 percent fewer new students started college.
Guess: They may not have been able to pay for it. College is expensive.
Advice: Young people should realize how important education is.
Conclusion: The government must not be providing enough financial aid.

D3: Working with Adverbs (p. 71)
Answers will vary.

D4: Writing Tip (p. 71)
Answers will vary.

CHAPTER 5

A3: After You Read (p. 75)
1. Answers will vary. Some examples are:
Sir Francis Galton's test tried to measure intelligence by examining the size and shape of a person's head.
2. Answers will vary. Some examples are:
Alfred Binet's original test had children perform tasks such as follow commands, name objects, and put things in order. Then he compared the children's performances.
3. Answers will vary. Some examples are:
The modern Stanford-Binet IV test is given orally. The examiner asks questions until no items can be answered correctly.
4. Answers will vary.

Examining Form (p. 53)
A.

SIMPLE PRESENT PASSIVE	SIMPLE PAST PASSIVE	PERFECT PERFECT PASSIVE	MODAL PASSIVE
is called are asked is given is examined	was based was proposed were developed were assigned	has been revised	could be used could be distinguished would be assigned can be answered

1. Simple present: The passive form has two words.
Simple past: The passive form has two words.
Simple present perfect: The passive form has three words.
Modal: The passive form has three words.
2. The form of the main verb is the past participle.
3. A form of *be* comes immediately before the main verb.
B. Answers will vary.

Examining Meaning and Use (p. 75)
1.	b	3.	a
2.	b	4.	b

B1: Listening (p. 78)
A.
1.	b	4.	b
2.	a	5.	a
3.	a	6.	a

B.
1.	b	4.	b
2.	b	5.	a
3.	a	6.	b

B2: Recognizing Passive Sentences (p. 79)
1.	—	6.	—
2.	✓	7.	✓
3.	✓	8.	✓
4.	—	9.	—
5.	✓	10.	✓

B3: Choosing Active or Passive Verb Forms (p. 79)
1.	have been given	6.	has been injured
2.	will have seen	7.	check
3.	are sent	8.	have been broken
4.	explain	9.	were asked
5.	was proposed	10.	understand

B4: Writing Active and Passive Sentences (p. 80)
2. The printer printed the document in under a minute.
The document was printed in under a minute.
3. The police are going to fine the driver $75.
The driver is going to be fined $75.
4. More comfortable seats have already replaced the benches in most train cars.
The benches have already been replaced by more comfortable seats in most train cars.
5. The visiting professor is supposed to give a lecture in the main hall today.
A lecture is supposed to be given by the visiting professor in the main hall today.
6. Someone must have left this package on my desk this morning.
This package must have been left on my desk this morning.

B5: Changing Sentences from Active to Passive (p. 81)
2. Three men who were driving a car through Oregon were stopped by police.
3. Can't be changed. "Laugh" and "fall" are intransitive verbs.
4. Can't be changed. "Suit" is a transitive verb with no passive form.
5. Patients are always encouraged to exercise by their doctors.
6. My mother was surprised and scared by the accident.
7. Can't be changed. "Weigh" is intransitive in this sentence.

8. The baby was weighed by the nurse.
9. Can't be changed. "Stay" is an intransitive verb.
10. By this time next year, all of the office computers will have been upgraded.
11. Can't be changed. "Cost" is a transitive verb with no passive form.
12. In fact, the problem could be solved.
13. An investigation is going to be opened early next year.
14. This problem may have to be talked about later.
15. Can't be changed. "Become" is a transitive verb with no passive form.

B6: Omitting or Including Agents (p. 81)

1. Mount Everest was identified as the world's highest mountain in 1852.
Unfortunately, all of these teams had been turned back by bad weather and the dangers of the high altitude.
2. In the United States, drivers' licenses are issued by individual states.
A passport, birth certificate, or a Social Security card are accepted as proof of identity by most, but not all, states.
3. The identity of the inventors of many everyday objects is not known.
Even today, the identities of inventors of world-changing items like the microchip are overlooked.
4. The answers to many basic questions can be found through a simple web search.
For more specific information, a variety of online databases can be consulted.

B7: Describing Processes (p. 82)

Answers will vary. Some examples are:
A. 1. The Melissa Virus was programmed into a Word document.
2. The document was then uploaded to an Internet newsgroup.
3. It was downloaded from the newsgroup site because it looked important.
4. When the document was opened, the virus was triggered.
5. Fifty new e-mails were created using the computer's address book.
6. The document was attached to these e-mails.
7. Then the e-mails were sent.
8. When these new e-mails were opened, 50 more e-mails were created.
9. These 50 new virus-infected e-mails were forwarded to 50 more people, and so on.
10. E-mail systems were overwhelmed, so they had to be shut down.
B. Answers will vary.

B8: Introducing Information Objectively (p. 83)

A. 2. It is being reported that tourism has increased in the region.
3. It is known that pollution is affecting many rainforests around the world.
4. It has been shown that this drug decreases the desire to smoke cigarettes.
5. Previously it had been thought that economy would recover quickly.
6. It is assumed that scientists will one day find a cure for cancer.

B. Answers will vary.

B9: Thinking About Meaning and Use (p. 84)

1. b   4. a
2. b   5. a
3. a   6. b

B10:   Speaking (p. 84)

Answers will vary.

C1: Editing (p. 85)

2. Is this book ~~been~~ *being* recommended for our class, or will it be required?
Has ~~Is~~ this book been recommended for our class, or will it be required?
3. Many of the scientist's ideas should ~~have not been~~ *not have been* dismissed by modern researchers.
4. The research team is now ~~being collected~~ *collecting* the data.
5. The results of the survey ∧*are* not going to be mailed until next week.
6. The winners were awarded scholarships and ~~gave~~ *given* positions as research assistants.
7. Only the top 10 percent of the class will be ~~offer~~ *offered* scholarships.

C2: Keeping the Focus (p. 86)

A. 1. The focus remains on "twin studies" throughout.
2. The second sentence is in the passive to keep the focus on twin studies.
B. 1. The focus shifts. The paragraph begins with a focus on "twin studies" and then shifts to "Sir Francis Galton." Then it shifts to "One of his methods" and then back to him.
2. The second sentence has no passive form.

C3: Organizing Information (p. 87)

2. yes
Today, he is recognized as one of the founders of modern educational philosophy.
3. no
Better in the active voice. The focus of the paragraph and sentence stays on the artists.
4. yes
Skinner was awarded a Ph.D. in 1931 by Harvard University.
5. yes
However, homework is expected by principals and even some parents to be a major part of the curricula.

C4: Writing Tip (p. 87)

Answers will vary.

CHAPTER 6

A3: After You Read (p. 91)

1. Agriculture, tourism, and technology
2. Answers will vary. Some examples are:
Traditionally the economy was based on agriculture. Today, the economy is strongly supported by tourism, and the opportunities in technology are growing.
3. Answers will vary.

Examining Form (p. 91)

A. Singular: information, democracy, tourism, steps, organization

Plural: advantages, bananas, cattle, monkeys, species

B. 1. No (information, tourism)
2. No (cattle)
3. species

Examining Meaning and Use (p. 92)

1. b
2. b
3. b

B1: Listening (p. 95)

A. For the past few ^years^, I've been visiting Costa Rica regularly for ^business^ and for ^pleasure^. My trips began when I had ^a chance^ to start ^a business^ there.
At that time, I quickly tried to find ^information^ about the Costa Rican economy. It was only by ^chance^, however, that I also found a perfect place for ^rest^, relaxation, and fun.

B. 1. b   4. a
2. b   5. b
3. b   6. a

B2: Contrasting Nouns (p. 96)

1. is   8. ideas
2. is   9. difference
3. those   10. was
4. were   11. takes off
5. has been   12. have been
6. sugar   13. are
7. are   14. don't

B3: Using Different Types of Nouns (p. 96)

Answers will vary. Some examples are:

1. art   7. *The National Review*
2. men, river   8. jury
3. New York   9. patience
4. group   10. parents
5. health   11. The History of Furniture, The New School
6. restaurant, lines 12. company

B4: Identifying Count and Noncount Nouns (p. 97)

A. 1. equipment: N   9. material: C
2. injury: C   10. speed: C
3. fun: N   11. knowledge: N
4. safety: N   12. movement: C
5. consumer: C   13. physics: N
6. research: N   14. information: N
7. use: C   15. advice: N
8. shape: C

B. 1. a. N   4. a. C
   b. C   b. N
2. a. C   5. a. N
   b. N   b. C
3. a. N   b. C

C. Answers will vary.

B5: Using Expressions with *Of* (p. 98)

A. Answers will vary. Some examples are:

an item of clothing   a pile of clothing
an item of news   a pile of mail
a piece of clothing   a sheet of ice
a piece of music   a sheet of music

B. 2. set of   5. pot of
3. bunches of   6. games of
4. pinch of   7. flash of

B6: Subject-Verb Agreement with Nouns (p. 98)

1. has, seems, explains, is
2. has, wants, thinks, is / are, is
3. is, show, have, threaten

Examining Meaning and Use (p. 99)

1. b   3. a
2. a   4. a

C1: Listening (p. 101)

A. Poor ^air quality^ is one of the major problems ^of^ well-insulated ^office buildings^. Fortunately, a ^low cost^ solution is ^widely available^. Studies show that ^houseplants^ help clean ^indoor^ air. They remove ^toxic chemicals^ and ^they also^ add oxygen. Plants ^with^ fuzzy leaves may also remove smoke and grease particles.

B. 1. b   4. a
2. a   5. a
3. b   6. a

C2: Using Adjective and Noun Modifiers (p. 102)

Answers will vary. Some examples are:

1. tall, handsome CEO
2. petite, fun-loving English teacher
3. multi-colored three-ringed plastic binders
4. extra-bright legal-sized paper
5. stocky young Caucasian
6. distinctive black and white wool cap
7. long, green diamond-studded gown

C3: Working on Compound Modifiers (p. 103)

A. 1. a first-floor apartment
2. a fifteen-minute presentation
3. a long-term commitment
4. a family-owned business
5. a two-way street
6. an 18-page instruction booklet
7. a small-business loan
8. a ten-dollar discount ticket
9. a strange-looking wild animal
10. the best-known college
11. a two-karat diamond
12. a world-famous artist

B. Answers will vary.

C4: Recognizing Adjectives vs. Compound Modifiers (p. 103)

3. The prize-^winning film was a Spanish movie called *The Sea Inside*.

4. OK

5. The group of skiers was caught in an unexpected ^and^ powerful avalanche.

6. The lamp was made of a strange-^looking yellow plastic.

7. OK

8. Beth is the most hardworking, supportive, and helpful volunteer we have.

10. OK

11. I just found a cool leather and chrome chair at the thrift store.

12. Some loud-mouthed guy interrupted the politician's speech.

C5: Using Compound Nouns (p. 104)

A.
2. show business
3. Global warming, fossil fuels
4. scuba diving
5. security guard
6. homework
7. flashlight, sleeping bag, camping trip
8. junk food, French fries

B.
2. takeout
3. greenhouse
4. storage unit
5. common sense
6. death penalty
7. food poisoning
8. solar system
9. mail order
10. sit-up

C. Answers will vary.

C6: Using Prepositional Phrases (p. 105)

A.
2. in
3. of
4. of
5. to
6. of
7. for
8. of
9. with
10. on

B.
1. I was stunned by the landscape's beauty.
4. I'm very lucky to have my parents' support.
8. Picasso's paintings have always confused me.

C. Answers will vary.

C7: Using Modifiers Effectively (p. 105)

Answers will vary. Some examples are:
1. Robbers broke into the Smith family's house last night and stole the family's computer.
2. A new world history book has been published by a history professor from Oxford University.
3. The meeting is with the university chancellor and the student government president.
4. The university's Journalism Department plans to hire several new faculty members.
5. The city council's public works committee has approved a one-million-dollar water-treatment facility.

C8: Working on Pronoun Agreement (p. 106)

1. it / they
2. they
3. them
4. it
5. It
6. it
7. them

C9: Thinking About Meaning and Use (p. 106)

1. b
2. a
3. b
4. b
5. b
6. b
7. a
8. b

C10: Speaking (p. 107)

Answers will vary.

D1: Editing (p. 108)

A local conservation team ~~have~~ _has_ received a three-~~years~~ _year_ grant to study the effects of urban development on local plant species. The first of the four phases ~~have~~ _has_ already been completed. The goal of phase one was to collect ~~informations~~ _information_. Phase two can now begin. It will require researchers to categorize the data from phase one. Plant growth, soil, and air quality ~~is~~ _are_ the main categories the team seeks to examine. Phase three will measure changes in the plants, soil, and surrounding ~~airs~~ _air_ over time. The final phase will involve analysis of these changes. The analysis ~~are~~ _is_ going to be used to plan wildlife preserves.

D2: Using Pronouns (p. 109)

Answers will vary. Some examples are:
2. The police raided several Internet cafés to gather evidence for their investigation. They said it would be used in an upcoming trial.
3. Famous fashion model Katie Krass will be throwing a huge party on the island of Ibiza to celebrate her upcoming wedding to rocker Johnnie Apples. The celebration will be held on Ibiza because she loves it and because she first met her fiancé there.
4. It seems that a group of world-renowned scientists cannot agree on how many planets there are in our solar system. They are meeting for a four-day conference in Belgium, where they will spend their time / the time discussing this issue.

D3: Writing Tip (p. 110)

Answers will vary.

CHAPTER 7

A3: After You Read (p. 113)

1. Answers will vary. Some examples are:
   There are many challenges as cities continue to grow, but we can make our city more livable by planning early.
2. Answers will vary. Some examples are:
   Key idea 1: Neighborhoods should be seen as places where we get new energy and life. They need to have all the services (like parks and libraries) that people need.
   Key idea 2: Walking is healthier for people and for cities. Walking should be encouraged by improving conditions like sidewalks and building "up" rather than "out."
   Key idea 3: We need to build more affordable housing so that people of all economic levels can live in the city. New taxes could be invested in the building of this housing.
3. Answers will vary. Some examples are:
   The tone of the manifesto is positive. There are descriptions of preventing negative consequences and ensuring a better tomorrow.
4. Answers will vary.

Examining Form (p. 114)

A.

A/AN	THE	Ø	OTHER DETERMINERS
a healthy neighborhood a public park a city	the news the construction the foot traffic the revenues	neighborhoods travel sidewalks	many challenges our advice its residents that trend this tax its friendly attitude affordable housing

B. Singular count nouns are used with *a/an*, *the* and other determiners. Plural and noncount nouns are used with *the*, no article, or other determiners.

Examining Meaning and Use (p. 114)

1. a
2. b
3. a
4. a

B1: Listening (p. 117)

A. ~~Recent~~ A recent study of ^the new housing in ^the area shows that there are many barriers to building affordable housing. Not only is there ^a lack of government subsidies, but there is also limited land for new construction in ^the region. Developers need tax credits that lower ^their debt on construction projects. ~~Subsidies~~ The subsidies allow them to offer lower rents to ^the public, and as ^a result, affordable housing becomes ^a reality.

B.
1. a
2. a
3. b
4. b
5. b
6. a

B2: Using *A/An* and *The* (p. 117)

1. e the
2. c The
3. a a
4. h the
5. b the
6. j the
7. f a
8. d a
9. g the
10. i a

B3: Reasons For Using Specific Nouns (p. 118)

A
1. the (Reason 2 and 4)
2. The (Reason 3 and 4), a
3. the (Reason 5)
4. a, a, the (Reason 3)
5. a, the (Reason 6), The (Reason 1), a

B. See answers above.

B4: Using Articles in Newspapers (p. 118)

A. Answers will vary. Some examples are:
2. The City Council is going to hold hearings on the latest scandal.
3. A major summer storm is going to hit the Cayman Islands.
4. A popular tourist destination has closed after an accident.

B.
1. A
2. an
3. Ø
4. Ø
5. a
6. Ø
7. a
8. Ø
9. Ø
10. the
11. the
12. A
13. the
14. a
15. the
16. a
17. the
18. the
19. Ø
20. the
21. the

B5: Contrasting Articles (p. 119)

A.
1. an, the
2. the, the
3. an, Ø, a
4. a, Ø, the
5. a, the, a
6. the, the
7. a, an
8. Ø, a
9. Ø, the, the
10. a
11. a
12. Ø, a, Ø

B. Answers will vary.

Examining Meaning an Use (p. 120)

1. b
2. b
3. a

C1: Listening (p. 121)

1. b
2. b
3. b
4. b
5. a
6. a

C2: Using Possessive Adjectives to Identify Specific Nouns (p. 122)

Answers will vary. Some examples are:

In 1914, Sir Ernest Shackleton placed this ad in a newspaper. He was looking for recruits for **his** expedition to the South Pole. The crew and **their/his** ship, the Endurance, would sail to the South Pole, where they would use **their** dogs to attempt the world's first crossing of the Pole by foot. In the end, they never even made it to the Antarctic continent. **Their** ship became frozen in ice in the Weddell Sea and **its** hull was crushed by the ice.

Using lifeboats, Shackleton and **his** crew sailed for seven days to Elephant Island. Later, Shackleton chose five men to sail one of the boats on to find help. Using primitive navigation equipment, they sailed for 17 days on the stormy seas and miraculously landed back where they had begun **their** journey—on the island of South Georgia.

But the story doesn't end there. Once on South Georgia Island, the six men hiked over glaciers and towering mountains to get help from a whaling station. They then sailed back to Elephant Island to rescue the remaining men. Twenty-two months had passed since they had left on **their** expedition.

The next time you are complaining because **your** airplane has been delayed for a few hours, remember that **your** inconvenience is nothing compared to what Shackleton and **his** men experienced!

C3: Using Demonstrative Adjectives to Identify Specific Nouns (p. 123)

A.
1. this
2. those
3. These
4. this
5. that
6. those
7. that
8. This

B.
1. We have many workers that are hired from overseas, and these foreign-born employees are good for our business. While Americans fill the majority of our jobs, the guest workers take those high-tech jobs

that Americans are not qualified for. They work hard, and we should welcome them to this country with open arms.

2. Do you remember that strike that took place last year? It had a huge impact on this industry. American workers require a certain salary and union benefits, whereas those guest workers at Carlton will work for less money and fewer benefits. That's why the corporations like to hire them. All I can say is that this problem is going to worsen before it gets better. And in the meantime, many well-educated Americans can't find work in this field.

C4: Working with Generic Nouns (p. 124)
Answers will vary.

C5: Connecting Information in a Paragraph (p. 125)
A. 5. Although the factors were changed, the employees' productivity appeared to increase each time a measurement was taken.

2. In 1927, Elton Mayo and two associates from the Harvard Business School decided to answer this question.

7. The workers felt satisfaction because both the researchers and their supervisors had taken an interest in them and because they had formed a sort of community with their co-workers during the course of the experiment.

4. Before the researchers took a measurement, they changed a different physical factor in the plant that might affect productivity (such as increasing or decreasing the temperature, light, or noise level.)

3. Mayo and his colleagues measured the productivity of a group of employees at the Hawthorne Works Electrical Plant in Illinois over a period of five years.

1. What physical conditions cause employees to be more productive?

8. This result, now known as "The Hawthorne Effect," demonstrates that social factors are more important than physical factors in motivating employees.

6. Surprised by these results, the researchers interviewed the workers and came to the following conclusion:

B. 5 "the factors" refers to "different physical factor in the plant" in sentence #4.

4 "the researchers" refers to Mayo and his colleagues in sentence #3.

6 "these results" refers to the increased productivity mentioned in sentence #5.

3 "his colleagues" refers to Mayo's two associates in sentence #2.

8 "this result" refers to the reason workers felt satisfaction in sentence #7.

C6: Thinking About Meaning and Use (p. 126)

1.	a. T	4.	a. T
	b. F		b. F
2.	a. F	5.	a. T
	b. T		b. F
3.	a. F	6.	a. F
	b. T		b. F

C7: Speaking (p. 126)
Answers will vary.

D1: Editing (p. 127)

Before leaving on my trip, I read *The Global Wanderer's Guide to Egypt*, ~~the~~ ᵃ useful guide to visiting that country. The first part of the book gives ᵃ̶ practical tips on traveling within Egypt. For example, travelers are told where to collect their bags at ~~an~~ the airport and given directions on how to get to ᵗʰᵉ Pyramids outside ᵗʰᵉ city of Giza. Other tips are directed at keeping healthy and comfortable: The book recommends carrying ᵃ bottle of water when touring in the heat and gives a̶n̶ advice on where to have tea in the afternoon. ~~A~~ The last part of the book deals with customs. For example, it reminds people that they must take off ~~the~~ their shoes before they enter a mosque. I highly recommend that you read this book before you plan ~~the~~ your trip to Egypt.

D2: Using Articles and Pronouns (p. 128)

A. 2. The city of Mumbai may seem overwhelming to Ø visitors at first. The city, located on the west coast, is the commercial and entertainment capital of India. It is also the most populous city. Recently, **the** population was reported to be more than 13 million.

3. The people of India speak many different languages. Although there are 15 official languages, its inhabitants can speak countless other languages and dialects. For Ø national, political, and commercial communication, however, they usually speak English or Hindi.

4. The Taj Mahal was built in the 17th century by **the** Indian emperor Shah Jahan as a tomb for his beloved wife, Mumtaz Mahal. The tomb was built on **the** banks of **the** sacred Jumna River near the medieval city of Agra. It was built from white marble.

B. Answers will vary.

D3: Writing Tip (p. 129)
Answers will vary.

CHAPTER 8

A3: After You Read (p. 133)
1. Answers will vary. Some examples are:
How many hours per week do people spend online?
A typical e-mail user spends 7–8 hours online.
What are people's main online activities?
A majority of e-mail users (52%) say that spending and receiving e-mail is their most common online activity.
How has e-mail affected people's use of the telephone and the U.S. Mail?
Many e-mail users say they now use the telephone and regular mail less than they used to, and about one in five indicate they use the telephone and regular mail "much less frequently."

2. Answers will vary.

Examining Form (p. 133)

QUANTIFIERS FOLLOWED BY COUNT NOUNS	QUANTIFIERS FOLLOWED BY NONCOUTN NOUNS	QUANTIFIERS NOT FOLLOWED BY NOUNS
both men and women almost all e-mail users each user a lot of users few differences some of the women many people quite a few users	some of the information both e-mail and the Internet a lot of time	some hardly any very few

A. 1. *Both*, *a lot of*, and *some* of are used with both count and noncount nouns.
  2. Quantifiers not followed by a noun are used as pronouns. They can stand alone because the noun is clear from the context.

B. Answers will vary.

Examining Meaning and Use (p. 134)

1. b
2. a
3. b
4. a

B1: Listening (p. 137)

A. ^Many^ Internet users shop online, especially adults who have ^little^ time to shop. ^The majority of online^ online shoppers are between the ages of 30 and 49. ~~Them~~ ^A lot of them^ appreciate the convenience and ^the large number of^ choices available online. ~~Seniors~~ ^Few seniors^ over age 65 shop online, although ^many^ would probably benefit from the convenience of purchasing ^some of^ their medications and groceries from home.

B. 1. a
  2. a
  3. b
  4. a
  5. b
  6. a

B2: Contrasting Quantifiers (p. 137)

1. much
2. a few
3. little
4. Lots
5. a little of
6. many
7. any
8. any
9. plenty of
10. some

B3: Quantifiers with Specific and Nonspecific Nouns (p. 138)

A. 1. –
  2. of
  3. –
  4. –
  5. of
  6. –
  7. of
  8. –
  9. of
  10. –
  11. of

B. Answers will vary.

B4: Making Comparisons with Quantifiers (p. 139)

A. Answers will vary. Some examples are:
  1. in cities
  2. crime

3. traffic
4. moving up in the world, chances to succeed
5. help around the house, do well in school
6. long hours on farms, do less physical labor
7. played simple games outdoors, sports, and expensive hobbies

B. Answers will vary.

Examining Meaning and Use (p. 140)

c Two members don't get tickets at all.
b All members get tickets.
a An individual member gets a ticket.
d Two members get tickets for themselves.

C1: Listening (p. 141)

A. Purchasing a computer nowadays often involves choosing ^either^ a laptop or a desktop model. ^Neither of these models^ is perfect for everyone's needs, and ^each^ ^has^ type ^certain^ shortcomings. It's important for ^every^ consumer to find out both the advantages and the disadvantages of ^each^ from the standpoint of price, quality, and need.

B. 1. b
  2. a
  3. b
  4. b
  5. b
  6. a

C2: Contrasting Quantifiers (p. 142)

1. both
2. neither
3. every
4. All
5. each
6. all
7. Each of
8. either
9. Neither
10. both

C3: Using *Each, Every, Both, Neither*, and *Either* (p. 142)

1. both
2. every
3. each
4. every
5. either
6. neither

C4: Using *of* (p. 143)

1. of
2. –
3. of
4. –
5. of
6. –
7. of
8. of
9. – / of
10. of

C5: Thinking About Meaning and Use (p. 143)

1. ✓
2. –
3. ✓
4. –
5. ✓
6. ✓
7. –
8. ✓
9. ✓

C6: Speaking (p. 144)

Answers will vary.

D1: Editing (p. 145)

1. Most ~~of~~ adults use a computer at home, work, or school.
2. Each ^student^ ~~students~~ registered for courses online.
3. My high school friends spent ^many / a lot of^ ~~much~~ hours text messaging.
4. You might be interested in some of ^the^ articles in this magazine.
5. Either answer ~~are~~ ^is^ correct.

6. There's a ~~few~~ _little_ space left in the closet for your clothes.

7. Neither of my brothers ~~do not have~~ _has_ children.

8. ~~Many~~ _Much_ of my e-mail is spam.

9. Hardly any of the students ~~didn't understand~~ _understood_ the lecture.

10. In general, most ~~of~~ users are happy with their e-mail providers.

D2: Using Pronouns (p. 146)

A.
1. c Several of them
2. f Some
3. a many of them
4. b A few
5. d most
6. e None of them

B. Answers will vary.

D3: Writing Tip (p. 147)

Answers will vary.

CHAPTER 9

A3: After You Read (p. 151)

1. The purpose of the research study was to determine the causes of overwork.
2. Answers will vary. Some examples are:
   Workers feel overworked because: (1) They have too many tasks at the same time and are interrupted often; (2) They have to do things that waste their time; (3) They have to be in contact with work during free time.
3. Answers will vary.

Examining Form (p. 151)

A.

Infinitives

In a sentence beginning with _it_: it's easy to overlook; It's difficult to get my work done on time.

Directly after a verb: tend to focus; asked to do; begin to blur the lines between work time and free time

After a verb + object: may be asking some employees to multitask too much

After an adjective: likely to be highly overworked

After a noun: the inability to focus on one's work; a very important skill to develop in today's economy

Gerunds

After a subject: Multitasking

Directly after a verb: try focusing on their jobs; have begun asking employees how strongly they agree with this statement; contact you to discuss work-related matters

After a verb + object: waste a lot of time doing tasks; have more difficulty focusing at work

After a preposition: a result of multitasking

B. Answers will vary.

Examining Meaning and Use (p. 152)

1. b I'll begin by making dinner after you arrive.
   a I'll begin making dinner before you arrive
2. b You helped him.
   a He helped you.

B1: Listening (p. 155)

A. Some employees can't imagine_^breaking_ all ties with work, even for a short vacation. They admit_^checking_ their voice mail

and even_^answering_ e-mails during vacation. Studies show, however, that employees need_^to relax_ and_^enjoy_ themselves on their vacations by fully_^removing_ themselves from work. Employees who can do this are much less likely_^to feel_ stressed when they return.

B.
1. b
2. a
3. b
4. b
5. b
6. a

B2: Contrasting Gerunds and Infinitives (p. 155)

1. studying
2. to take
3. coordinating
4. saying
5. to file
6. to run
7. having
8. to win
9. to discuss
10. answering
11. fixing
12. singing
13. to stop, doing
14. to be hiding

B3: Verbs Followed by Gerunds and Infinitives (p. 156)

A.
1. a. eating
   b. to eat
2. a. to call
   b. calling
3. a. seeing
   b. to see

B. Answers will vary.

B4: Completing Sentences with Gerunds and Infinitives (p. 156)

Answers will vary.

B5: Changing Gerunds to Infinitives (p. 157)

A. <u>Having constant food cravings can be very unsettling</u>. <u>Changing your eating habits</u> First, <u>learning the triggers for your cravings</u> is very helpful. In addition, <u>occupying your mind with other thoughts</u> can be helpful. Finally, if you must eat something, <u>substituting healthy foods for fatty ones</u> is a smart move.

B. It can be very unsettling to have constant food cravings. It takes a lot of discipline to change your eating habits. It is very helpful to learn the triggers for your cravings. It can be helpful to occupy your mind with other thoughts. It is a smart move to substitute healthy foods for fatty ones.

B6: Verbs Followed by Object + Infinitive (p. 157)

Answers will vary. Some examples are:
1. b. Don't look at anyone else's paper during the test.
   ⟶ She warned us not to look at anyone else's paper during the test.
2. a. Sit down. ⟶ He ordered his dog to sit down.
   b. Roll over. ⟶ He told his dog to roll over.
3. a. Please help me with the dishes. ⟶ She asked him to help her with the dishes.
   b. Let's go shopping. ⟶ She invited him to go shopping.
4. a. You should be kind to other people. ⟶ They advised them to be kind to other people.
   b. Finish your homework. ⟶ They urged them to finish their homework.

B7: Performer of an Action (p. 158)

A.
3. Your calling every day means a lot me.
4. I don't like her bossing everyone around all the time.
5. I can't tolerate your playing music at all hours. OR I can't tolerate you playing music at all hours.
6. My parents' allowing me to attend the party was a lucky turn of events. OR Their allowing me to attend the party was a lucky turn of events.

B.
2. It takes too much time for her to walk to work.
3. It's convenient for her to pick up the kids in the afternoon.
4. I advised him not to go on the trip.
5. I encouraged them to tell the truth.
6. It's not a good idea for you to be friends with Kelly.

C. Answers will vary.

Examining Meaning and Use (p. 159)

1. b We don't want to make calls.
   a We don't want to get calls.
2. b I left.
   a I might leave.
3. b She'll announce the results.
   a Someone will tell her the results.
4. b The exam is tomorrow.
   a The exam was yesterday.

C1: Listening (p. 160)

1. a
2. b
3. b
4. b
5. a
6. a
7. a
8. b

C2: Using Passive Gerunds and Infinitives (p. 161)

A. Being overworked
to be challenged
to be done
being told
to be
evaluated
Being treated
to be solved

B. Answers will vary.

C3: Perfect Infinitives and Gerunds (p. 162)

A.
1. to have disappeared
2. having taken
3. having seen
4. to have left
5. not to have understood
6. to have committed
7. to have caught
8. having conducted
9. to have indicated
10. to have carried

B.
3. However, he does remember seeing the painting . . .
4. can't rewrite
5. At first, he pretended not to understand . . .
6. can't rewrite
7. The police were happy to catch Mr. White, . . .
8. After conducting a thorough examination . . .
9. Clues found at the scene seem to indicate . . .
10. can't rewrite

C4: Thinking About Meaning and Use (p. 163)

A.
1. Same
2. Different
3. Same
4. Same
5. Different
6. Different
7. Same
8. Same
9. Same
10. Different

C5: Speaking (p. 163)
Answers will vary.

D1: Editing (p.164)

Work-centric people focus almost exclusively on their work life. Dual-centric people, on the other hand, tend ~~focusing~~ *to focus* on both their families and their work. They enjoy working with colleagues as well as ~~to stay~~ *staying* at home with their families. Most "dual-centrics" say they want to work hard, play hard, and enjoy life.

The big question is how do dual-centric people manage to balance their lives so well? Setting a strict boundary between home life and office life ~~are~~ *is* obviously one strategy. They do this by ~~taking not~~ *not taking* phone calls from the office while they are at home. They also take time off. When they decide *to* go on vacation, they take it—no matter what.

Interestingly, although dual-centric people usually work fewer hours, they don't have fewer responsibilities on the job. They are just as productive as other workers, but they have decided to set and ~~keeping~~ *keep* boundaries between work life and home life.

D2: Referring to Gerunds and Infinitives (p. 165)

A.
2. Walking to work   d   it
3. Hiring smart people and giving them a large budget and complete freedom   a   this business model
4. to travel around the world   b   it
5. To achieve my goal of finishing a marathon   f   The experience
6. Choosing a suitable career   e   this challenge

B. Answers will vary.

D3: Reporting Opinions and Ideas (p. 166)

A.
2. The average commute is estimated to take 45 minutes.
3. The number seven is believed to be lucky.
4. Prices are expected to rise dramatically.
5. Spiders and other insects are thought to be helpful.
6. Parents are said to be too permissive these days.

B. Answer will vary.

D4: Writing Tip (p. 167)
Answers will vary.

CHAPTER 10

A3: After You Read (p. 171)

1. Answers will vary. Some examples are:
The purpose of the article is to discuss some of the more personal details about Einstein's life that are less familiar.
2. Answers will vary.
3. Answers will vary.

Examining Form (p. 171)

1. Nouns modified by highlighted clauses are:
<u>Einstein's incredible intellect</u> that captured the public's imagination, . . .
<u>the hundreds of books about him</u> that are currently in print, which include several published in the past year alone.
details about <u>his life</u> that you may not know.
<u>a mild personality disorder or a learning disability</u> which affected his speech.
<u>a child</u> whose interests included playing the violin and listening to classical music
<u>his school</u>, where success was determined by one's ability to memorize facts
<u>mathematics, and in Latin</u>, which he respected because of its emphasis on logic.
<u>a playful man</u> who was easy to talk to . . .
<u>his cousin Elsa</u>, whom he eventually married.
<u>Eduard</u>, who excelled in the arts, . . .
2. The different relative pronouns in these clauses are *that*, *which*, *whose*, *where*, *whom*, and *who*.
3.

RELATIVE PRONOUN + VERB	RELATIVE PRONOUN + SUBJECT + VERB
that captured the public's imagination which include several published in the past year alone which affected his speech who was easy to talk to who excelled in the arts	that you may not know whose interests included playing the violin and listening to classical music where success was determined by one's ability to memorize facts which he respected because of its emphasis on logic whom he eventually married

B. Answers will vary.

Examining Meaning and Use (p. 172)

1. b This sentence is about a person.
   a This sentence is about a book.
2. a You have to make some calls.
   b Some students have to make some calls.
3. a We have one TV.
   b We have more than one TV.

B1: Listening (p. 175)

A. In both ancient and modern times, the idea of dreams
has been something~that~captures peoples' imaginations.
A dream is a series of images, events, and feelings~which~
occur in your mind while you are asleep. In ancient
times, dreams were believed to be messages the
gods sent to warn people about the future. In 1900,

Sigmund Freud,~who~is considered the father of modern
psychology, published a famous book~which~is called *The
Interpretation of Dreams*. Today, people still believe
they have dreams~in which~information about the future is
revealed. Moreover, there are numerous reports of artists
and inventors~whose~dreams inspire them, and many actually
keep notebooks~where~they record their dreams.

B. 1. a   3. a   5. b
   2. b   4. a   6. b

B2: Contrasting Subject and Object Relative Clauses (p. 176)

1. were   6. are
2. you are   7. I bought
3. you got   8. happened
4. aren't   9. I am
5. we were   10. I hadn't

B3: Combining Sentences (p. 176)

A. 2. Free speech is a freedom which many people in the United States take for granted.
   3. A storm which hit the U.S. state of Florida in 2004 caused millions of dollars in damage.
   4. The job was given to another man who had been at the company for only one year.
   5. They are a really good group of workers who we appreciate and respect a lot.
   6. The city built a light-rail system which connects the suburbs and downtown.

B. All of the sentences can be rewritten using *that* as a relative pronoun.

B4: Writing Definitions with Relative Clauses (p. 177)

A. Answers will vary. Some examples are:
   1. A generous person is someone who does good things for other people.
   2. A best friend is a person that you can call at any time—day or night.
   3. A good job is one that pays well and gives you satisfaction.
   4. A classic book is one that everyone should read.
   5. A home is a place which makes you feel comfortable and happy.
   6. A good teacher is a person who can explain things well.
   7. A museum is a place that houses great art.
   8. A holiday is a time that people visit their families.

B. Answers will vary.
C. Answers will vary.

B5: Other Relative Pronouns (p. 177)

A. Answers will vary. Some examples are:
   1. I remember the day when my sister was born.
   2. I know a great restaurant where you can get delicious mussels.
   3. Two thousand and one was the year when I started school.
   4. Someday I'd like to live in a place where I'm not cold all the time.
   5. I don't know the reason why I dislike my boss.
   6. Taipei is a city where you can stay out all night.

B. Answers will vary.

B6: Object Relative Clauses with Prepositions (p. 178)

A.
1. e   Immigration is an issue that/which I'm very concerned about.
2. a   Einstein is a famous person from history that/who I'd like to have a conversation with.
3. f   Physics is an academic subject that/which I excel in.
4. d   Rio de Janeiro is a city that/which I would like to live in someday.
5. c   Acting and writing are two jobs that/which I'm well suited for.
6. b   My birthday is an event that/which I always get excited about.

B.
1. Immigration is an issue about which I'm very concerned.
2. Einstein is a famous person from history with whom I'd like to have a conversation.
3. Physics is an academic subject in which I excel.
4. Rio de Janeiro is a city in which I would like to live someday.
5. Acting and writing are two jobs for which I'm well suited.
6. My birthday is an event about which I always get excited.

C. Answers will vary.

B7: Omitting Relative Pronouns (p. 178)

1. Television is an invention ~~that~~ we cannot credit to a single inventor.
2. The ideas ~~that~~ many inventors come up with can appear strange to people that aren't inventors.
3. The person **who** invented the ballpoint pen was a Hungarian journalist.
4. There's a new book about Thomas Edison ~~which~~ I've read **that** I highly recommend.
5. Guglielmo Marconi was the inventor ~~whom~~ I think invented the radio.
6. Elias Howe was the inventor **who** created the sewing machine and the zipper.
7. Many men and women ~~who~~ we think of as our greatest inventors were considered strange by their colleagues.
8. The light bulb and the phonograph are the inventions ~~that~~ Thomas Edison is most famous for.

B8: Contrasting Relative Pronouns (p. 179)

1. that / who
2. where / in which
3. whose
4. that / which
5. whose
6. which
7. who / whom / Ø
8. where
9. who
10. who
11. to whom
12. that / when / Ø

B9: Restrictive and Nonrestrictive Relative Clauses (p. 179)

A.
2. I have one older brother, **who lives in Los Angeles.**
3. He is an actor **who you may have seen** in several TV commercials.
4. My sister, **whose family recently moved to Dallas,** is only ten months older than me.
5. She lives in a housing development **where almost everyone works for the same company.**

6. My twin brother, Marcus, is the one **who I'm the closest to.**
7. My neighbor has an old van **that always breaks down.**
8. Our family reunion, **which happens every other year,** is always a lot of fun.

B. Answers will vary.

C. Answers will vary.

B10: Using *Which* to Modify a Clause (p. 180)

A.
1. I told my mother I'd go shopping with her today, which means I won't be home until late.
2. My computer isn't working, which is going to make it hard for me to finish my work.
3. The board meets regularly on the first Tuesday of the month, which isn't very convenient for me.
4. My sister forgot to pick me up again today, which proves she's not very responsible.
5. We're going to go to dinner instead of a movie, which is what I wanted to do in the first place.
6. The professor is giving us an extra week to finish our papers, which is exactly what I hoped she would do.

B. Answers will vary. Some examples are:
1. I lost my cell phone this morning, which is extremely annoying.
2. I have to catch up on my homework, which means I'm not going to be able to go out all weekend.
3. The weather is supposed to be terrible today, which is going make it hard to work outside.
4. The movie doesn't end until midnight, which means I'll get home very late..

Examining Meaning and Use (p. 181)

1. ✓ The guy was rude.
2. ✓ You should speak to one person.
3. ✓ My necklace is from Brazil.

C1: Listening (p. 182)

A. Personal data assistants, ∧called PDAs, are handheld electronic devices ∧designed to help busy working people. These small devices, now ∧considered essential by many in the business world, have become extremely versatile. The models ∧made by all leading manufacturers help users perform many tasks ∧including browsing the Internet, sending and receiving e-mail, playing computer games, and even making phone calls. A person ∧using a PDA, therefore, may have a dozen electronic tools ∧available at the same time.

B.
1. b   4. a
2. b   5. b
3. b   6. a

C2: Adding Information with Appositives (p. 183)

A.
2. The telegraph, a machine for transmitting written information by wire, sends information using a coded series of dots and dashes.
3. One of the foundations of modern biology is the work of Charles Darwin, the naturalist who proposed the theory of natural selection.

4. Linguistics, the scientific study of human language, was first recognized as an academic discipline in the early 1800s.
5. Unlike the Olympics, the X Games, an event featuring action sports, are held every year.
6. The United Nations, an international organization founded in 1945, aims to facilitate cooperation between countries.

B. Answers will vary.

C3: Using Adjective Phrases (p. 183)

Anyone who ~~looks~~ (looking) at that symbol of the modern age, ~~which is~~ the skyscraper, can easily tell (that) ~~it~~ wasn't the idea of a single person. Rather, the skyscraper is the result of a series of technical innovations <u>that ~~were~~ made in many fields over the course of many decades</u>. First, in the mid-19th century, a process <u>that ~~allowed~~ (allowing) steel to be produced inexpensively</u> was developed by William Kelly, ~~who was~~ <u>an American</u>, and Henry Bessemer, ~~who was~~ <u>an Englishman</u>. Cheap steel made it possible to build structures higher than had been done with traditional materials. Reinforced concrete, <u>which uses steel bars to strengthen the material</u>, was also used. Moreover, since most people find it difficult to climb more than six stories of stairs, the development of the elevator was another innovation (that was) <u>essential for the building of skyscrapers</u>.

The engineering <u>~~that was~~ required to build skyscrapers</u> was in place by the middle of the 1880s, when the Home Insurance Building in Chicago, <u>~~which was~~ the world's first skyscraper</u>, was built. Initially, the architectural styles <u>~~that were~~ used in the design of these tall buildings</u> imitated past eras, such as the Renaissance. However, in the 20th century, a style developed <u>that many people most strongly associate with the skyscraper</u>—art deco. This style, <u>which reached the height of its popularity in the 1920s-1930s</u>, represented a forceful modern belief in the promise of the future. The Chrysler Building and Empire State Building, <u>~~which are~~ two of the most famous skyscrapers in New York</u>, were built in the art deco style.

A new type of building <u>which ~~belongs~~ (belonging) to the "skyscraper family"</u> is the next step in skyscraper development. Called "superscrapers," these buildings are even taller and are being constructed using the latest technological advances. One example of a superscraper is the Burj Dubai building in Dubai.

C4: Combining Sentences (p. 184)

A. Answers will vary. Some examples are:
2. Many runners, exhausted from their efforts, collapsed before they reached the finish line.
3. The meeting determining the winner was held in secret. OR The meeting, held in secret, determined the winner.
4. I saw a strange object flying across the sky.
5. The runner up, hoping to win the contest, was very disappointed.
6. We think the plan suggested by the group leader is good.
7. You can get help at the Writing Center, located on the lower level of the library.
8. My boss, an avid car collector, just bought an original Model T built in 1908.

C5: Thinking About Meaning and Use (p. 185)

1. b   5. b
2. a   6. b
3. b   7. a
4. a

C6: Speaking (p. 185)

Answers will vary.

D1: Editing (p. 186)

1. There are several people in my class who ~~is~~ (are) planning to major in English.
2. Last year, I visited the Grand Canyon, ~~that~~ (which) I found awe-inspiring.
3. Radium is the invention ^(for) which Marie Curie is famous. OR Radium is the invention which Marie Curie is famous ^(for).
4. The hardware store did have the tools that I needed ~~them~~ to repair my bicycle.
5. My friend, ^(who) you met yesterday, told me about a new restaurant.
6. Architects ^(who / that) use space creatively are always in great demand.
   Architects ~~use~~ (using) space creatively are always in great demand.

D2: Introducing Paragraphs (p. 187)

A. Answers will vary. Some examples are:
2. The United Nations is an organization that works to reduce global conflicts.
3. The Louvre, which is located in Paris, is the best museum I know.
4. Living in foreign country is an experience that you never forget.
5. Nature preservation areas are places where endangered species can be protected.

B. Answers will vary.

D3: Writing (p. 188)

Answers will vary.

CHAPTER 11

A3: After You Read (p. 191)

1. Answers will vary. Some examples are:
   Conflict resolution in animal groups is sometimes necessary because the size of the group must be maintained.
2. Answers will vary. Some examples are:
   The loser, winner, or third party may initiate conflict resolution.
3. Answers will vary. Some examples are:
   When they raised the stumptail and rhesus monkeys together, they discovered that the stumptail had a positive influence on the rhesus monkeys' behavior.
4. Answers will vary.

Examining Form (p. 191)

A.

CONNECT IDEAS IN A SINGLE SENTENCE	CONNECT IDEAS BETWEEN SENTENCES OR PARAGRAPHS
yet so but and	most importantly for instance however like furthermore in fact nevertheless on the other hand

B. Answers will vary.

Examining Meaning and Use (p. 192)

c   The second clause is a bit surprising or unexpected.
a   The two clause show choices.
d   The second clause is a result of the first.
b   The second clause tells why the first clause is true.

B1: Listening (p. 194)

A. A day at the zoo may be a treat for you *, but* is it really paradise for the animals? This is a controversial issue *, so* let's look at the some of the most important pros and cons. Zoos provide food and shelter for animals *, and* they protect endangered species. These may sound like good ideas in theory *, yet* what actually happens at many zoos is another matter. Are the animals being protected *, or* are they being kept from their natural environment? There is no simple answer *, nor is there* a simple solution. We're just asking you to think about it. For more information, contact your local animal rights advocacy group.

B.
1. b   4. a
2. a   5. a
3. a   6. b

B2: Contrasting Conjunctions (p. 195)

1. and   6. so   11. and, for
2. but   7. yet   12. nor
3. nor   8. so
4. yet   9. so
5. or, but 10. but, and

B3: Connecting Ideas (p. 195)

A. Answers will vary. Some examples are:
1. and it's expensive.
   but I want to try it anyway.
   so I don't think you should try it.
2. for it is affecting my health.
   or I want lose some weight.
   so I'm going to join a support group.
3. nor did he have his passport.
   yet they still let him on the flight.
   so they wouldn't let him on the plane.
4. or you could try to help yourself.
   but you should also make sure that everyone is OK.
   and you could stay there until help arrives.

B. Answers will vary. Some examples are:
1. I don't like to eat meat, but sometimes I can't avoid it.
   I don't like to eat chocolate, nor do I like ice cream.
2. In my free time, I enjoy swimming, and I also like golf.
   In my free time, I enjoy swimming, but I never have time to do it.
3. I think it's important to save money, for it provides security.
   I think it's important to save money, yet I almost never manage to do it.
4. In the next year, I might start my own business, so I want to apply for a loan.
   In the next year, I might start my own business, or I may go to a graduate school.

B4: Omitting Words in the Second Clause (p. 196)

My best friend and I decided to take a vacation together. At first, we couldn't decide what to do: spend time at the beach or ~~spend time~~ in the mountains. After much discussion, we settled on a cruise through the Virgin Islands. The plan was to fly to St. Thomas, ~~and to~~ do some quick sightseeing, and ~~to~~ board the cruise ship.

The night before our departure, I washed ~~my clothes~~, and packed my clothes. My brother called me at around midnight ~~and he~~ wished me a safe journey.

On the day of our flight, my friend and I were very excited. However, when we got to the airport, we found out that our flight was overbooked, and the next one didn't leave for 48 hours. Taking the later flight would mean that we'd miss our ship's departure from St. Thomas.

Although I'm usually a patient person, this time I lost my temper. After all, it wasn't our fault. We hadn't checked in late nor ~~had we~~ forgotten our tickets or passports. We'd gotten our tickets months in advance‸ and ~~we had~~ confirmed our seats on the flight. After much discussion, we decided to buy tickets on a different airline so we could get to St. Thomas in time. The new tickets were not cheap!

Now it's three months later, yet we're still arguing with the airline. They have apologized‸ and ~~they have~~ offered to give us a $50 travel voucher or ~~to give us~~ a rental car coupon, but we want a complete refund. We haven't yet been reimbursed for our unused tickets‸ but ~~we~~ still hope that it will happen. The vacation was wonderful‸ but ~~it was~~ also very expensive!

Examining Meaning and Use (p. 197)

c a contrasting idea
e a time relationship
a a similarity
d a result
b more detailed information

C1: Listening (p. 201)

A. ‸Like any‸ ~~Any~~ close-knit group in the animal kingdom, people who work together don't always get along. ‸In fact, a‸ ~~A~~ majority of managers cite employee conflicts as a major problem. Training employees in conflict resolution‸, therefore,‸ has become a big business itself. One Seattle conflict resolution center‸, for instance,‸ reports that business has tripled over the last five years. "It's not that employees are fighting more," says director Mark Mason. "‸On the contrary, they're‸ ~~They're~~ just more aware that something can and should be done about workplace conflicts."

B. 1. a   4. a
    2. a   5. a
    3. b   6. a

C2: Contrasting Transition Words (p. 201)

1. However
2. For example
3. Most importantly
4. As a result
5. Moreover
6. Because of this situation
7. Similarly
8. in fact
9. Despite this

C3: Connecting Ideas (p. 202)

Answers will vary. Some examples are:
1. Similarly, if you don't exercise, you will also gain weight.

2. As a result, I'm exhausted most of the time.
   Despite this, I've still managed to find time for my friends.
3. At the same time, you'll lose fat.
   Most importantly, you'll look and feel better.
4. On the contrary, many patients report that it doesn't hurt at all.
   Because of this, they are afraid to try it.
5. Likewise, many smaller businesses have faced problems as well.
   However, they have also benefited from increased opportunities.
6. First, you should make sure you are well rested.
   For example, you could look for a low-stress job.
7. Moreover, I've also talked about what to do during the interview.
   In conclusion, the main point is that you must do your research thoroughly before the interview.

C4: Connecting Information in a Paragraph (p. 203)

A. 7 First, elephants are known to be very compassionate.

3 Also, dolphins, like humans and chimpanzees, have demonstrated this ability to a limited degree.

6 Recently, scientists decided to begin work with elephants. "Why elephants?" you may ask.

10 Next, they put Happy in front of a mirror, where she began to touch the tip of her trunk to the X mark on her face.

1 We all know that human beings can recognize themselves in a mirror.

13 However, some scientists remain skeptical of the research and its results, saying that it is too simplistic.

4 Scientists are always looking for other mammals to study that demonstrate self-awareness. The problem is that most animals are obviously not intelligent enough to recognize themselves in a mirror.

11 Furthermore, Happy seemed to be following her own movements in the mirror as if she was mesmerized. She was recognizing the image in the mirror as her own.

2 Similarly, chimpanzees have been shown to exhibit the same level of self awareness.

14 Despite this negativity, the researchers who worked with Happy remain optimistic and have pledged to do further testing with the elephants.

9 To begin the tests, scientists gave an elephant named Happy a "mark test." They painted a white X on her right cheek. The mark would be visible to her only when she looked in a mirror.

8 In addition, their large brains make them intelligent candidates for this kind of test.

5 Dogs, for example, will bark at their own image in a mirror—thinking it's another dog. They have no sense of self-recognition.

12 This research about self-awareness and recognition around Happy and other elephants has generated a great deal attention in the press and the scientific world.

B. Answers will vary. Some examples are:
Paragraph 1: 1, 2, 3, 4, 5
Paragraph 2: 6, 7, 8
Paragraph 3: 9, 10, 11
Paragraph 4: 12, 13, 14

C5: Thinking About Meaning and Use (p. 204)

1.	a	6.	a
2.	b	7.	b
3.	a	8.	a
4.	b	9.	b
5.	a	10.	b

C6: Speaking vs. Writing (p. 205)

Answer will vary.

D1: Editing (p. 206)

1. Scientists have studied and ~~have~~ demonstrated the great capacity of the chipanzee for both learning and teaching.

2. Humans pass down knowledge and traditions from parents to children; ^likewise, chimpanzees train, ~~likewise,~~ their offspring in particular behaviors. . . .

3. Researchers presented the same problems in two groups of chimps. The first group found one set of solutions to the problems✗ meanwhile, the second group devised completely different solutions. . . . OR
   Researchers presented the same problems to two groups of chimps. The first group found one set of solutions to the problems, ^Meanwhile, ~~meanwhile,~~ the second group devised completely different solutions.

4. Previous studies suggested that chimps simply conform to the behaviors of the group, but new research conflicts with that idea, ~~however~~. OR
   Previous studies suggested that chimps simply conform to the behaviors of the group, ^. New ~~but new~~ research conflicts with that idea, however.

5. "It's quite meaningful," said Dr. Feagan, a lead researcher. "Chimps ^can learn and ~~can~~ transmit knowledge over many years. This helps us gain a deeper understanding of early human history."

6. Chimpanzee culture is quite sophisticated; ^however / in contrast ~~in addition,~~ other primates do not share such complex social organization.

7. Chimpanzees have a complicated communication system. ^Therefore, scientists ~~Scientists~~ can learn, ~~therefore,~~ a great deal from observing them in the wild. OR
   Chimpanzees have a complicated communication system. Scientists can ^therefore, learn, ~~therefore,~~ a great deal from observing them in the wild.

D2: Choosing Conjunctions vs. Transitions (p. 208)

Answers will vary. Some examples are:

1. In the 1980s, business managers began recognizing that competition was hurting productivity, so they sought ways to encourage collaboration. Personality testing was introduced to help employees understand themselves and each other. In addition, workshops on conflict resolution became popular in large companies and organizations.

2. Dogs are territorial creatures and will fiercely defend their own territory against other animals. However, dogs usually behave differently when they are in neutral territory. They typically get along well with other dogs when they meet in public.

3. It is true that children can be taught ways to work out their differences, but young children can be quite immature. Therefore, experts teaching conflict resolution only after a child can speak well.

4. When experts examined the brains of birds, they did not see physical signs of intelligence. They therefore assumed that birds were not intelligent. New technology, however, offers much improved brain imaging. In fact, recent research shows that birds are smarter than was previously thought.

5. Professor Logan became a celebrity after his appearance on a television talk show. However, he has always been a serious scholar. For example, he has earned three research grants and published two articles just in the past two years. Because of this, he is well qualified to head the committee.

D3: Indicating Point of View (p. 209)

2.	Unfortunately	5.	strangely / ironically
3.	Incredibly	6.	unexpectedly
4.	Coincidentally		

D4: Writing Tip (p. 209)

Answers will vary.

CHAPTER 12

A3: After You Read (p. 213)

1. Pre-exam rituals mentioned include: (1) Taking a meat cutlet to school on the day of an exam; (2) eating candy bars around exam time; (3) using brand new or hand-me-down pencils during an exam; (4) not shaving during exam week; and (5) wearing the same perfume while studying and during an exam.

2. Dr. Foley's main point is that students who engage in pre-exam rituals may do better on their exams. Dr. Lewis's main point is that we need to relieve exam anxiety so that students won't have to engage in pre-exam rituals.

3. Answers will vary.

4. Answers will vary.

Examining Form (p. 213)

A. Before he leaves home
   although the words for *meat cutlet* and *to win* are written differently
   While there is no proof that the chocolate bars do anything
   Wherever there are students being tested,
   because they have never been used to write or erase

any mistakes
so that he can harness their "lucky power" on his exam
while they are studying for their finals
Once they arrive at the exam hall
although exam superstitions can be fun and even
beneficial

Examining Meaning and Use (p. 214)

1. a
2. a
3. b

B1: Listening (p. 217)

A. *Even though my*
~~My~~ brother denies it, he's really quite superstitious. For

example, he always puts a lucky charm in his pocket $_\wedge$ *before*

Once a
he leaves for an exam. ~~A~~ soccer tournament begins, he

so that
won't shave. He stays home on Friday the Thirteenth $_\wedge$

he can avoid bad luck. And of course, he won't walk

because
under a ladder $_\wedge$ he's sure that's asking for trouble.

Whenever he's
~~He's~~ asked about this behavior, he says he's just being

careful, not superstitious!

B.
1. b		4. b	
2. b		5. b	
3. a		6. a	

B2: Contrasting Subordinators (p. 217)

1. when
2. Even though
3. while
4. Since
5. so that
6. As
7. until
8. when
9. in order to
10. Though
11. because

B3: Showing Time (p. 218)

A.
1. learned
2. stuff / are stuffing
3. said / was saying
4. read / have read
5. hits
6. finish / have finished
7. improved
8. are chopping / chop
9. entered
10. be
11. is sent / will be sent
12. come / are coming

B. Answers will vary.

B4: Giving Reasons and Showing Concession (p. 219)

A. Answers will vary. Some examples are:
2. Although I would want to help, I don't think I could lie.
3. I wouldn't date someone ten years older than I am because I don't think we'd have a lot in common.
4. Since I have a family to take care of, I could never work for 80 hours a week.
5. I'd rather be poor and happy because I think happiness is more important than wealth.

B. Answers will vary.

B5: Combining Sentences (p. 219)

2. b While Joe is about five foot six, his brother Josh is over six feet tall.
3. g I took the day off from work so that I could see my son's piano recital.
4. h You can see the stage clearly wherever you sit in the theater.

5. a Since you're walking there at night, you shouldn't go alone.
6. f She passed the test even though she had a fever.
7. c I want to buy a personal computer so that I can work from home.
8. e While I was coming to work today, I saw a horrible accident.

B6: Replacing Adverb Clauses with Prepositional Phrases (p. 220)

Answers will vary. Some examples are:
2. Because of a knee injury, he can't go dancing anymore.
3. We're going to dinner after the movie.
4. I got extremely thirsty while running in the marathon.
5. Despite her hard work, she did not receive the promotion.
6. The after-school program has been canceled because of a funding cut.

B7: Completing Sentences with Adverb Clauses (p. 220)

A. Answers will vary. Some examples are:
1. Everywhere I went on my last vacation, I bought a souvenir.
2. I went to college to study music so that I could teach elementary school music.
3. Although I don't like it when people forget my name, it's sometimes understandable.
4. Because I made a resolution to exercise more, I've joined a gym.
5. Wherever you go in Paris, you can find wonderful restaurants.
6. You should study harder in order that you might do well in school.

B. Answers will vary.

B8: Answering Question Using Adverb Clauses (p. 221)

Answers will vary. Some examples are:
2. After the book came out, the media reported on the book's claims and called it the Mozart effect.
3. While some hospitals started giving out classical music CDs, some schools were required to play classical music.
4. Every newborn was given a CD so that they could listen to it and become more intelligent.
5. Although some scientists support the research, others are skeptical.
6. Despite the fact that the Mozart effect hasn't been proven, some parents still believe in it.
7. We won't know the truth until more research is done.

Examining Meaning and Use (p. 222)

1. b		3. b	
2. b		4. a	

C1: Listening (p. 224)

A. *Having just picked up*
~~Just~~ our new car, my father parked outside our house.

admiring
I stood there in awe, $_\wedge$ every inch of it. Then without

warning, a shower of salt landed on the car. I looked

just as
around $_\wedge$ my mother's hand was returning to her pocket

rushing *while explaining*
for more salt. "Stop," yelled my father, $_\wedge$ to her side $_\wedge$

Not interested, my
how the salt would damage the paint. ~~My~~ mother

Deciding not
insisted that bad luck could damage it more. ~~Not to~~

challenge this superstition, my father permitted her to throw more salt ~~.~~ *. Though surprised at* my father's reaction, I was glad that

our new car would be "protected!"

B. 1. a   4. a
2. b   5. a
3. a   6. a

C2: Reducing Adverb Clauses (p. 225)

Showing Time

2. can't be reduced
3. ✓ Since winning the World Cup, the team has given many interviews.
4. ✓ When not winning Olympic medals, she's busy volunteering at her favorite charity.
5. can't be reduced
6. ✓ Upon/On reaching the top of the mountain, the hikers drank a lot of water.

Giving Reasons

7. ✓ Being injured, she had to forfeit the match.
8. can't be reduced
9. ✓ Having never given a speech before, he's very nervous. or Never having given . . .
10. ✓ Knowing that I liked sweets, they gave me a box of chocolate.
11. can't be reduced

Showing Concession

12. can't be reduced
13. ✓ Though planning a trip to Italy, they hadn't begun to save money for it.
14. ✓ Though not dating anyone special, I have gone out a couple of times recently.
15. ✓ Although not trying to make me angry, he's managed to offend me twice!
16. ✓ Although difficult, swimming is wonderful aerobic exercise.
17. can't be reduced

C3: Omitting Subordinators in Adverb Phrases Showing Time (p. 226)

2. ✓ Getting into a taxi, Eliza dropped her cell phone in the street.
3. can't omit the subordinator
4. ✓ Having exercised at the gym on my lunch break, I went back to the office.
5. can't omit the subordinator
6. ✓ Having learned English, she has better job opportunities.
7. ✓ Leaving the hotel, he was stopped by a security guard.
8. ✓ Looking through some old papers, I found a photo of my mother as a girl.

C4: Using Adverb Phrases (p. 227)

Mike Pierce was interested in the Antarctic. Years ago, *while studying the history of the area* ~~while he was studying the history of the area~~, he became

interested in the daring exploits of the early explorers to the South Pole. *Having read the exciting stories about their trips to the South Pole* ~~After reading the exciting stories about their trips to the South Pole~~, he decided he wanted to

have his own adventure in that cold wasteland. That desire led him to participate in a marathon run that was held in Antarctica last year. *Upon finishing the run and returning from his trip* ~~When he finished the run and he returned from his trip~~, he knew that he wanted to go back.

When it was announced that there would be another race this year, he jumped at the opportunity to participate.

This year's race will be longer: It's a double marathon (100 kilometers). Mike is one of only two runners from the previous year's race who will be returning to the Antarctic to compete. *Having completeed a marathon there before* ~~Because he has completed a marathon there before~~, he knows how challenging it can be. He's taking four layers of clothing, which he will wear at all times during the race. *Although excited about the physical challenge* ~~Although Mike is excited about the physical challenge~~, Mike is not returning to the South Pole simply because of the race. He's going back because he's fallen in love with the place.

It's not going to be easy, though. While he's running across the snow and ice, the environment will provide many challenges. It will be windy, lonely, and of course, cold. However, the one thing he won't he won't have to worry about is sunlight. There will be plenty of it, as the sun never sets this far south.

Training for the upcoming race has proven to be a challenge. *Not having anywhere cold enough to train for his run* ~~Since Mike doesn't have anywhere cold enough to train for his run~~, he has had to think creatively. To address this problem, he's called up businesses, asking if he could rent space in their walk-in freezers for training purposes. *Thinking he was a prank caller* ~~Because they thought he was a prank caller~~, most of the people he called hung up on him. However, one person listened to his story and then agreed to let him do it.

Mike will be leaving soon to head down south. *Before departing* ~~Before he departs~~, he will undoubtedly be thinking about his next adventure. Rumor has it that he'd like to cross the entire Antarctic sometime in the near future. *Knowing the degree of his determination and drive* ~~Because we know the degree of his determination and drive~~, we won't be surprised if he reaches that goal!

C5: Correcting Dangling Participles (p. 228)

Answers will vary. Some examples are:

2. Since I wasn't paying attention, the ball hit me in the face. OR Not paying attention, I was hit in the face by the ball.

3. After we took a break, the meeting continued. OR Having taken a break, we continued the meeting.

4. Because it was in a horrible condition, I needed to do a lot of work on the house. OR Being in a horrible condition, the house needed a lot of work.

5. Though I wasn't looking for a job, my old company made a generous offer to me. OR Though not looking for a job, I received a generous offer from my old company.

6. While I was walking back home yesterday, a car nearly hit me. OR Walking back home yesterday, I was nearly hit by a car.

C6: Thinking About Meaning and Use (p. 229)

1. ✓	5. –	9. –
2. –	6. –	10. ✓
3. –	7. ✓	
4. ✓	8. ✓	

C7: Speaking (p. 230)

Answers will vary.

D1: Editing (p. 231)

Even thought rock climbing is dangerous, more and more people are taking up the sport. When you are rock climbing, you are trying to get from the bottom to the top of a rock. Although this description sounds quite simple, ~~but~~ there is a lot more to it. One of the main tasks for a climber is to stay out of danger, ~~Because~~ *because* it is quite easy to fall and injure yourself.

Near the ground, most rocks have many handholds—cracks and outcrops—so even an amateur can usually climb smaller rocks easily. However, after ~~climbed~~ *climbing* for a while, you usually find the rock becoming smoother, and the handholds getting farther apart and smaller. At this point, you are not only higher but also in a more dangerous position. Because the terrain becomes challenging, ~~so~~ you must take safety measures—primarily by using safety ropes.

While / When / As ~~Though~~ you are climbing, you should try to do most of the work with your legs. Ideally, you should keep your body centered over your feet so that you stay balanced. By keeping your feet directly beneath your body, you can use the strength of your legs to push upwards. In certain cases, you must spend a great deal of energy ~~in order to~~ *so that* you can move just a few inches, but most climbers say that it is worth it. *Upon / After* ~~As~~ reaching the top of a difficult rock, a climber often feels a sense of euphoria.

D2: Connecting Ideas (p. 233)

Answers will vary. Some examples are:

Acknowledging Other Opinions

1. **While** some designers <u>do not like to work on computer</u>, most modern designers have welcomed the change.

2. **Although** some people argue that <u>it's a waste of time / it's a fad / its popularity won't last</u>, most people who meditate regularly report positive results, such as stress relief and an improvement in overall health.

Restating an Idea Already Introduced

3. **Before** <u>starting a race</u>, they drink plenty of water, but they do not eat any solid food.

4. **When** <u>writing an academic paper</u>, students must reference all material from other sources.

Giving Background Information

5. **Because** <u>there are now so many cable channels</u>, TV networks must be very creative in order to attract viewers.

6. **However**, although teamwork <u>is not usually taught / emphasized in school</u>, it's something most employers value highly.

D3: Using Concise Language (p. 234)

Answers will vary. Some examples are:

Because ~~In light of the fact that~~ rabies is both deadly and agonizing, many people believe that more should be done to prevent it from spreading. Rabies is a disease spread through the saliva of certain animals. *When* ~~In a situation in which~~ someone is bitten by a rabid animal, he or she must seek immediate treatment. About 72 hours *after* ~~subsequent to~~ being bitten, the symptoms begin to take hold and they cannot easily be reversed. Symptoms begin with flu-like feelings which then lead to disorientation and a loss of mental control. *While* ~~Despite the fact that~~ a lot of money has gone into researching rabies, scientists still know very little about the disease.

D4: Writing Tip (p. 235)

Answers will vary.

CHAPTER 13

A3: After You Read (p. 239)

1. The three topics are the moon, asteroids, and stars.
2. Answers will vary.
3. Answers will vary.

Examining Form (p. 239)

A.

PRESENT IN THE *IF* CLAUSE	If you see an object in the sky that isn't twinkling, that probably means it's a planet, not a star.	
PRESENT IN THE MAIN CLAUSE		
PAST IN THE *IF* CLAUSE	If there were no Moon, there would be no lunar tides.	If the moon didn't exist, the Earth would be spinning much faster.
MODAL IN THE MAIN CLAUSE		
PAST PERFECT IN THE *IF* CLAUSE	If XPR-209 had hit the Earth, it would have caused extensive damage.	If it had collided with our planet, we might have survived.
PAST MODAL IN THE MAIN CLAUSE		

B. Answers will vary.

Examining Meaning and Use (p. 240)

1. a
2. b
3. a
4. b

B1: Listening (p. 244)

A. ~~You~~ *If you* drive a hybrid car, you get better gas mileage and you create less carbon dioxide and other pollution. ~~You~~ *Even if you* can't afford a hybrid, however, there *are* still things that every car owner can do. First, if you get regular tune-ups, then *you'll get* better gas mileage and you'll pollute the air less. Second, *you'll* also get better mileage *if* you *keep* your tires properly inflated. Finally, drive at a medium speed *whenever* you can. ~~Your~~ *If your* engine works harder than necessary, it *burns* more gas and *creates* more emissions.

B.
1. b
2. a
3. b
4. a
5. b
6. a

B2: Using Present Real Conditional: Timeless (p. 244)

A.
2. d If you are orbiting above the Earth, the Great Wall of China is the only visible manmade structure.
3. e If you cross the International Date Line, you lose or gain a day.
4. f If an earthquake causes a violent shift on the ocean floor, a tsunami can happen.
5. a If the Moon temporarily blocks the Sun in the sky, it's called a solar eclipse.
6. b If you eat late at night, the food in your stomach immediately turns into fat.
7. c If you tap the top of a soda can, it stops the contents from foaming.

B. Statements 1, 2, 6, and 7 are false.

B3: Using Future Real Conditionals (p. 245)

A.
2. b If you unplug electronic devices that you're not using, you'll save on your utility bill.
3. f If you plant shade trees around your home, you'll reduce your air conditioning bill.
4. a If you buy food from local farmers, you'll keep money in your community.
5. d If you form a carpool with coworkers, you'll help cut down on air pollution.
6. c If you take fewer showers, you'll lower your water consumption.

B. Answers will vary.

B4: Using Conditionals with Modal Forms (p. 245)

A. Answers will vary. Some examples are:

Possibility
2. If Nancy is late for the meeting, she might be stuck in traffic somewhere.
3. If Joe has to work through lunch, he may not be able to eat at all.
4. If Tina's computer keeps crashing, it could have a virus.

Advice
5. If you can't finish your homework now, you'd better do it later.
6. If you are exhausted, you should take a break.
7. If you are unhappy in your current job, you should look for a new one.
8. If you wake up early tomorrow, you can help me make breakfast.

B. Answers will vary.

B5: Using Mixed Time Real Conditionals (p. 246)

Answers will vary. Some examples are:
If he enjoyed Paris, he's going to love Prague.
If he ate something spoiled, he probably doesn't feel very well today.
If he was off last week, he'll have to work a double shift next week.
If he was out late last night, he's probably pretty tired today.
If he wasn't at school yesterday, he may be out of town.
If he committed the crime, he'll be convicted.

B6: Using Alternatives to *If* (p. 247)

A.
2. You can't take Biomedical Ethics unless you've completed Introduction to Critical Thinking.
3. You can take Brain, Mind, and Behavior only if you have three credits in psychology or biology.
4. You can take Intermediate Algebra providing that you have a strong mathematics background.
5. You can take Introduction to Critical Thinking even if you don't have a philosophy background.
6. You can't take Principles of Psychology unless you are a first-year student.
7. You can take world religions as long as you are a religious studies major.

B. Answers will vary. Some examples are:
2. You shouldn't buy an expensive home unless you can afford the mortgage payments.
3. It's OK to get a large dog providing that you have a large home.
4. You should go back to school for a second degree only if it will help you to get a better job when you graduate.

5. You shouldn't skip class, even if it is boring.
6. You can give money to charity as long as you have enough money to pay your bills.

C. Answers will vary.

Examining Meaning and Use (p. 248)

1. a
2. b
3. a

C1: Listening (p. 250)

A. Do you ever wonder what ~would have~ happened ~if~ you had acted differently at some important point in your life? ~Would your~ Your whole life ~have been~ different? What would your life ~be~ like now? ~If you had~ You the chance, ~would~ you go back and make changes? Many people think they ~wouldn't make~ the same mistakes again. They act ~as though~ they ~know~ all the right answers now. Well, I'm not so sure.

B.
1. b   4. a
2. b   5. a
3. b   6. b

C2: Present/Future Unreal Conditionals (p. 251)

A. Answers will vary. Some examples are:
2. If I were you, I'd start by studying a little bit each day.
3. If I were you, I might get a tutor.
4. If I were you, I'd ask for a raise.
5. If I were you, I wouldn't go on the date.
6. If I were you, I'd sell it and start taking public transportation.

B. Answers will vary.

C3: Omitting *If* Clauses (p. 251)

Answers will vary.

C4: Using Past Unreal Conditionals (p. 252)

A. Answers will vary. Some examples are:
2. If she hadn't tripped, she could have won the race.
3. If it hadn't rained, the wedding would have been held outdoors.
4. If she hadn't answered the final question correctly, she wouldn't have won a new car.
5. If he hadn't known CPR, she could have died.
6. If I hadn't worked on a farm when I was a teenager, I might not have become a veterinarian.
7. If they hadn't won three matches in a row, the game wouldn't have ended quickly.
8. If my realtor hadn't given me bad advice, I wouldn't have lost money when I sold my house.

B. Answers will vary.

C5: Using Mixed Time Unreal Conditionals (p. 252)

A. Answers will vary. Some examples are:
2. If I were good at math, I could have become an astronomer.
3. If I hadn't won the lottery, I wouldn't be living in Beverly Hills now.
4. If I hadn't lost my wallet, I wouldn't be spending time buying a new one.
5. If I didn't like to photograph old temples, I wouldn't have visited Angkor Wat last year.

6. If my car hadn't broken down, I wouldn't need to take the bus to work everyday.

B. Answers will vary.
C. Answers will vary.

C6: Using *As if* and *As though* (p. 253)

A.
2. e   4. h   6. c   8. f
3. b   5. a   7. d

B. Answers will vary. Some examples are:
1. My older brother bosses me around as if he's my father.
2. I didn't recognize her, but she said "hello" as though we had met before.
3. While we were in France, she acted as though she could speak French, even though she only speaks English.
4. I was so hungry that I felt as if I could eat everything on the table.
5. He's so critical of other people. He behaves as though he's never made a mistake.
6. Due to the blizzard, our three-hour bus trip took seven hours. It seemed as if it was the longest journey of my life.
7. When I heard the news about the car accident I felt as though I would faint.

C7: Thinking About Meaning and Use (p. 254)

1. b   4. b   7. a   10. a
2. a   5. a   8. b   11. b
3. a   6. b   9. a   12. b

C8: Speaking (p. 255)

Answers will vary.

D1: Editing (p. 256)

1. You should read The Worst-Case Scenario ~if~ if you want to learn how to survive in different bad situations.
2. ~You should back away slowly if~ ~If you should back away slowly~, you need to escape from a mountain lion.
3. The lion will pay more attention to you if you ~will~ try to run from it.
4. You ~would~ *will* suffer an internal injury if someone ~*punches*~ you hard in the stomach.
5. However, you can protect yourself from injury, ~if~ *if* you tighten your stomach muscles.
6. If I ~will~ get a raise, I'll definitely save more money.
7. ~If you hear three shots,~ ~You hear three shots~ if it means the race has begun.
8. If you need more money ~*,*~ I can lend you some.
9. ~Whenever~ *If* I had paid attention last semester, I would have passed the course.
10. I would take a trip abroad if I ~would have~ *had* some vacation days left.

D2: Working on Implied Conditionals (p. 258)

A.
2. The program could have worked if people had followed the rules.
3. If people don't visit their doctors regularly, serious problems can go undetected.
4. If people don't have good eating habits, they risk serious health problems.

5. If people don't recycle the garbage they create, there won't be enough places to dump it all.
6. Her presentation would have been more impressive if she had prepared thoroughly.
7. If the legislation had been passed, it would have helped clean the air.
B. Answers will vary.
C. Answers will vary.

D3: Writing Tip (p. 259)
Answers will vary.

CHAPTER 14

A3: After You Read (p. 263)
Answers will vary. Some examples are:
1. E-waste consists of electronic items (such as cell phones and computers) that are thrown away.
2. E-waste ends up in landfills. Many electronic devices contain toxins that can learch into the soil and the groundwater.
3. Consumers throw away the devices because they break more easily and because advertisers encourage them to buy new ones all the time.
4. One solution is for consumers to donate their computers and other items for recycling. Another solution could be for companies to build sturdier electronic devices.

Examining Form (p. 264)
A.

THAT CLAUSES	
IN A SENTENCE BEGINNING WITH *IT*	that many of today's electronic devices are "made to break"
AFTER *BE*	that most people don't think twice about tossing even large electronic items that many electronic parts are extremely toxic
AFTER A VERB	that you throw away your home telephone every other year that 20 million computers a year are discarded in the United States alone that they are built less sturdily than they were a generation ago
AFTER A NOUN	that it won't harm the environment
WH- AND *IF/WHETHER* CLAUSES	
AS A SUBJECT	Whether Vanessa needs a new cell phone or not
AFTER A PREPOSITION	how to recycle their hardware
AFTER A VERB	what happens to your old cell phones and computers where they are going if recycling is even possible
AFTER AN ADJECTIVE	what happens to your old cell phones and computers

B. Answers will vary.

Examining Meaning and Use (p. 264)
1. b   3. b
2. a   4. b

B1: Listening (p. 268)
A. We admit it, *Whether we or not* our reliance on electronic equipment is ruining the environment. *The belief that* That new equipment is better and faster means *that* consumers are filling garbage dumps with an unprecedented amount of toxic waste from discarded electronics. As a consumer, it is essential that you *be* aware of this problem. Here are some suggestions about *what you can* do:
1. Find out *where* your local electronic recycling center *is*.
2. Decide *whether or not* you can repair or upgrade your old equipment.
3. Challenge *the idea that* newer is always better.

B.
1. a   4. b
2. a   5. b
3. a   6. a

B2: Identifying Noun Clauses (p. 268)
It was with high hopes that this reviewer attended the opening night production of *Henry* at Broadway's Limelight Theater. Unfortunately, the show did not live up to my expectations. I found myself wondering aloud why I had bought a ticket to see it. In a nutshell, I thought that *Henry* was terrible.

The play is supposed to be a comedy. However, one of the main problems was that the script simply wasn't funny. The person sitting next to me actually fell asleep—twice. In addition, the plot was difficult to follow because of to poor writing. For example, by intermission it wasn't clear if the leading couple knew each other, yet by the end of the play they were getting married!

Of course, I may not have been able to hear everything. The Limelight was renovated last year, but the acoustics remain a problem. It's often difficult to hear what's happening on stage. The actors need to speak up or they need better microphones!

One other problem was the costumes. Although the play is supposed to take place in the 19th century, the actors costumes looked surprisingly modern. How the director didn't notice this is a mystery to me.

I think the producers should listen to how the audience responded at the end of the show—with lukewarm applause at best. I suggest that they go back to the drawing board on this one: the script needs a complete revision and the two leading actors should be replaced.

So, when it comes to seeing *Henry* on Broadway, don't worry about whether you're missing a good production or not. Trust me: you're better off saving your money and using it for something else—like a good dinner with friends.

B3: Introducing Noun Clauses (p. 269)
1. Where
2. that
3. where
4. whether
5. That
6. when
7. that
8. how
9. that
10. if
11. what
12. that
13. whose
14. why
15. what
16. when

B4: Combining Sentences (p. 270)

Answers will vary. Some examples are:

2. We realized that the ground was shaking.
3. I don't know if I can tell you the answer.
4. I can't read what that sign says.
5. Who is going to win hasn't been determined yet. OR It hasn't been determined yet who is going to win.
6. That we don't have enough money is a problem. OR The problem is that we don't have enough money. OR It's a problem that we don't have enough money.
7. I want hear about what you saw while you were on vacation.
8. I'm not certain if he has the time to help me.

B5: Using *That* Clauses After Verbs (p. 270)

A. Answers will vary. Some examples are:

2. I suppose that their lifestyles changed a lot. When you win that much money, you can afford to do a lot of new things.
3. I think most of the lottery winners probably took exotic vacations. That's what I would do.
4. I would guess that they moved into bigger houses.
5. I don't believe that they moved to new areas. Most people want to stay where their family and friends live.

B. Answers will vary.

B6: Using *Wh-* Clauses and *If/Whether* Clauses (p. 271)

A. Answers will vary. Some examples are:

2. Question: Are we meeting tomorrow or not?
   Noun clause: I'm confused about whether we're meeting tomorrow or not.
3. Question: Are you going to attend the party?
   Noun clause: I'd like to know if/whether you're going to attend the party.
4. Question: Did you leave your keys in the car?
   Noun clause: I wonder if/whether you left your keys in the car.
5. Question: Did you turn off the lights?
   Noun clause: I can't remember if/whether you turned off the lights or not.

B. Answers will vary. Some examples are:

2. Question: Which language does she speak?
   Noun clause: It depends on which language she speaks.
3. Question: How did Alexander Fleming discover penicillin?
   Noun clause: We learned about how Alexander Fleming discovered penicillin.
4. Question: Why were they absent?
   Noun clause: We need to find out why they were absent.

B7: Using *Wh-* Clauses as Subjects (p. 272)

Answers will vary. Some examples are:

2. What this means is that the birth rate is not high enough to replace an area's population.
3. Why this has happened is because more women live in cities and work outside the home.
4. Where this is the biggest problem is Hong Kong, Singapore, Ukraine, and Lithuania.
5. How this issue could be solved is if families were given money to have bigger families.

B8: Using Infinitives in Place of Noun Clauses (p. 273)

2. It's essential for you to pack some sturdy walking shoes.
3. I have to ask you to tell the truth. Do I need to get in better shape for the trip?
4. The hills are very steep, so I advise you to exercise and to get in shape.
5. I don't know how to get there.
6. It's necessary to travel by train. There are almost no cars in the villages.
7. I can't decide when to go.
8. I advise you to avoid the high season in the summer. It's very crowded then.
9. I wonder how long to stay.
10. It's best to stay a few nights. That way you can spend one whole day in the area.

B9: Completing Sentences (p. 273)

A. Answers will vary. Some examples are:

2. It's important that we talk about what we're doing for your birthday.
3. I truly believe that voting is important in a healthy society.
4. What frustrated me most when I first studied English was that I couldn't pronounce anything well.
5. I'm concerned about whether or not I'll do well on my finals this semester.
6. I find it annoying that my friends don't keep in touch better.
7. The problem with cell phones is that people abuse them.
8. It's obvious that convenience and affordability are an important part of American culture.
9. There is a possibility that I'll be going to Italy this year.
10. Some people think I'm not very nice. The truth is that I'm shy.

B. Answers will vary.

B10: Thinking About Meaning and Use (p. 274)

2.	Different	7.	Different
3.	Same	8.	Same
4.	Different	9.	Same
5.	Different	10.	Same
6.	Different		

B11: Speaking (p. 275)

Answers will vary.

C1: Editing (p. 276)

Are video games too violent? Do they provide any benefit? I believe ~~what~~ that today's debate about video games is actually nothing new. During my childhood, radio was what my brother and I listened to ~~it~~ for entertainment. Even then, my grandmother was worried that we were being exposed to too much violence, so she suggested that my mother ~~didn't allow~~ not allow radio in the house.

However, I remember spending many wonderful afternoons sitting next to my brother listening to whatever show was on that day. It was not a problem (for us) that we could not

see the images. The sound effects were so well-done ^that we
could picture everything perfectly. ~~What did we do~~ *What we did* was use
our imaginations. And when the show was over, we would
go outside and pretend we were the characters.

   Computer video games tap into the imagination in a
similar way. My nephew loves to play video games. What
engages his mind is not whether or not ~~can he see~~ *he can see* the
picture. It's his imagination that he uses to direct the
events of game. After finishing a game, he often goes
outside and plays with his friend—just like I did.

C2: Condensing Information and Clarifying Ideas (p. 277)

A. 2. At the end of the day, many travelers to foreign
       countries do not know what they will eat, where they
       will sleep, or how they will pay for their next ticket.
   3. Historians are still wondering if the great Mayan
      culture declined because of environmental causes
      or if social and political issues caused its decline.
   4. In the United States, it is inappropriate to ask an
      acquaintance how old you are, how much money
      you make, or how much you weigh, as these are all
      considered private.
   5. Anthropologists disagree about many questions
      such as whether or not early humans first appeared
      in Africa, and if tool-making was responsible for an
      increase in human brain capacity.
   6. When choosing a career, it is important to identify
      what tasks you are good at, what environment you
      enjoy, and what sort of rewards you expect.

B. Answers will vary. Some examples are:
   2. What this implies is that there are certain occasions
      when it is OK to lie.
   3. What this suggests is that they are not exercising or
      eating a healthy diet.
   4. What we can conclude is that global warming is a
      real phenomenon.

C3: Making Objective Comments (p. 278)

Answers will vary. Possible answers:
   2. It is widely assumed that power corrupts people.
   3. It is thought that city people are unfriendly.
   4. It was once assumed that smoking was perfectly safe.
   5. It is well-known that exercise improves one's energy.
   6. It is understood that reading is a pathway to
      intelligence.

C4: Writing Tip (p. 279)

Answers will vary.

CHAPTER 15

A3: After You Read (p. 283)

Answers will vary. Some examples are:
   1. The writer feels that a little lie is not as bad as a big
      lie. He gives the examples of: friends lying to you to
      spare your feelings versus someone who lies about
      killing someone.

   2. People often touch their nose when they are lying.
      They also cross their arms, laugh inappropriately, lean
      forward, use hesitations, and lick their lips.
   3. The polygraph was invented because we are not good
      at detecting liars. However, it cannot tell us who is a
      liar. It can only tell us that a person is stressed.
   4. Answers will vary.

Examining Form (p. 284)

A.

PRESENT IN THE REPORTING CLAUSE	PAST IN THE REPORTING CLAUSE
researchers say that there might well be a connection between lying and the nose on your face Researchers studying mendacity explain that most of us try to dupe someone at least once a day. They also say that we frequently try to find out whether others are deceiving us. Some say it is an invaluable tool, others reply that nothing could be further from the truth They warn that a polygraph cannot and never will tell us who's a liar.	Michel de Montaigne said that lies came in all sorts of shapes and sizes. They told you how delicious your cooking was. They asked politely whether you could give them the recipe. he informed the police that he did not do it Carlo Collodi warned the young that lying could make their noses grow longer with each lie they told. Hirsch told *USA Today* that when people were lying, the tissue in the nose began to fill with blood, causing swelling. Hirsch also said that people's stuttering rate and errors in speech increased when they weren't telling the truth.

B. Answers will vary.

Examining Meaning and Use (p. 284)

   1. We asked Maria a question.
   2. The computer hasn't been repaired yet.
   3. Luis went home the day he said this.
   4. I need to call Jim's boss.

B1: Listening (p. 288)

A. A man ^said that ^he ^loved his birthday gifts. In fact, he was really
   disappointed with them. A child watching TV ^assured her father ^that she
   ^had completed ^her homework. She really hadn't. A woman ^told a caller that ^she had to
   get off the phone because the doorbell was ringing. It
   wasn't! Psychologists ^say ^that these are all lies. They ^claim ^that
   if a person intends to be misleading, then he or she is
   lying. Indeed, psychologists ^admit ^that these are small lies,
   often called "white lies," but since they ^are ^all attempts to
   deceive, they still fall under the category of lying.

B. 1. b   4. a
    2. b   5. b
    3. a   6. a

B2: Identifying Reported Speech (p. 289)

   1. —   6. —
   2. ✓   7. ✓
   3. ✓   8. —
   4. —   9. ✓
   5. ✓   10. —

B3: Choosing Reporting Verbs and Introducing Reporting Clauses (p. 289)

1. told
2. said
3. told
4. said
5. asked
6. if
7. that
8. when
9. that
10. what

B4: Choosing Verb Forms in Past Tense Reporting (p. 290)

1. b
2. a
3. b
4. b
5. b
6. a
7. a
8. b
9. b
10. a

B5: Making Other Changes in Reported Speech (p. 290)

1. she
2. they
3. her
4. him
5. our
6. his
7. earlier
8. the next day
9. that day
10. the day before

B6: Writing Quoted Speech (p. 291)

A. Answers will vary. Some examples are:
2. "What have you learned about life?"
3. "I was dancing when I lost my necklace."
4. "I'll call you today."
5. "You must talk to me if you have any problems." OR "You have to talk to me if you have any problems."
6. "You can use my phone any time you need it."

B. Answers will vary. Some examples are:
2. She asked if I had eaten in the new cafeteria yet.
3. They said/told me that they had discussed the question with their boss a week earlier.
4. He asked what I was going to do if I had to move.
5. She asked if I could believe that she used to live there.
6. He said/told me that she could arrive any time the next day.

B7: Keeping the Same Verb Form (p. 291)

A. 1. I said I would take the purple sweater, but they gave me the red one! (must change verb form)
3. He asked me what my grandfather was like. (past informal report)
4. The experts have all told us that global warming is a serious matter. (general truth)
5. B: He said you need to hurry! The train's coming into the station. (immediate report)
6. But my mother said if I really wanted to go, I could use her car. (must change verb form)
7. I wanted to ask Jill a question, but she said she didn't have the time to talk. (must change verb form)
8. She asked me if I'm going to see Angelo soon. (future event)

B. Answers will vary.

B8: Using Other Reporting Verbs (p. 292)

Answers will vary. Some examples are:
2. He questioned whether I was really committed to my job.
3. She explained (to me) that you have to log on first, and then enter a password.

4. She suggested that I see a dentist about my tooth.
5. He replied that he'd love to take on the project for me.
6. He insisted that I accept his gift.

B9: Changing Demonstrative Adjectives and Pronouns (p. 293)

Answers will vary. Some examples are:
2. He said my cartoons/the cartoons on my desk were the funniest he'd ever seen.
3. She wondered if the jeans she was wearing looked big on her. She asked whether her jeans looked big on her.
4. She thought the dress I was wearing looked gorgeous. She said my dress was gorgeous.
5. Scott asked me to read the application he was about to send in. Scott asked if I could read the application he was working on before he sent it in.

B10: Paraphrasing in Reported Speech (p. 294)

Answers will vary. Some examples are:
2. Joe asked if he could start a project later because he had a vacation booked. Jill said OK. Joe wondered if it would be OK if he started the project later because he had a vacation booked. Jill said it wouldn't be a problem.
3. Jill asked Joe if she should marry José. Joe said she should. Jill asked Joe whether or not she should marry José. Joe said that José is great and Jill should marry him.
4. Jill asked what Joe thought of her suit. He said he liked the blue one better. Jill wasn't sure if she liked her new suit and asked Joe. He said that he thought she looked better in the blue one.
5. Joe asked if Jill had gotten a job she had interviewed for. Jill said her experience was perfect, so they offered it to her. Joe asked Jill whether she got the job. Jill said she had because her experience had been perfect and they offered her the job right there.

B11: Present Tense Reporting (p. 295)

2. Some experts claim that people only use ten percent of their brains.
3. Liz says she has to look for a new apartment.
4. My brother admits he didn't go to my ball game last night.
5. Your boss tells me you're doing very well at your job.
6. My mother explained that she used to ski, but she doesn't anymore.
7. My sister admits she lost my CD,
8. Doctors tell us that fatty foods are bad for us,

B12: Thinking About Meaning and Use (p. 296)

1. F
2. T
3. F
4. ?
5. F
6. F
7. ?
8. T

B13: Speaking (p. 296)

Answers will vary.

C1: Editing (p. 297)

I recently saw a program on TV about a new exhibit on traditional textiles and fabrics. The interviewer, a young man, was talking with the exhibit curator and asked what did the exhibit include *included* besides things like blankets and clothing. The curator explained, "~~That~~ *that* because traditional textiles are rich in symbolism and color, they had had a significant effect on certain artists. She told *him* that because of this influence, the exhibit also included works by painters who had been influenced by woven designs. I remember thinking at the time, "That's very thought-provoking. I'd love to see this exhibit." Then, the interviewer added that entrance to the exhibition was included with the regular museum admission fee, and asked the curator did she think *if* she ~~think~~ *thought* more people *would* visit it for that reason? The curator responded ~~him~~ that the museum never charges additional fees for special exhibitions because they want as many people as possible to enjoy them. I can't wait to see it.

C2: Using Alternatives to Reporting Verbs (p. 299)

A. Answers will vary. Some examples are:
2. According to my brother, the movie was awful.
3. Sociologists once made the claim that women were less intelligent than men.
4. My parents have often made the assertion that honesty is the best policy.
5. In my favorite teacher's view, any dream can come true if you have the courage to pursue it.
6. Andy Warhol, the notable artist, once made the observation that everyone will be famous for fifteen minutes.

B. Answers will vary.

C3: Writing Tip (p. 299)

Answers will vary.